TERRITORIAL MASONRY

The Story of Freemasonry and the Louisiana Purchase

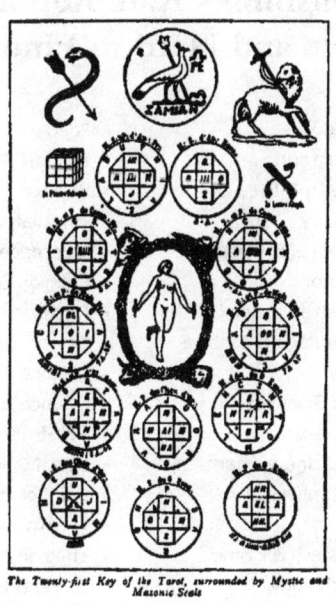

The Twenty-first Key of the Tarot, surrounded by Mystic and Masonic Seals

Ray V. Denslow

Kessinger Publishing's Rare Reprints
Thousands of Scarce and Hard-to-Find Books!

- Americana
- Ancient Mysteries
- Animals
- Anthropology
- Architecture
- Arts
- Astrology
- Bibliographies
- Biographies & Memoirs
- Body, Mind & Spirit
- Business & Investing
- Children & Young Adult
- Collectibles
- Comparative Religions
- Crafts & Hobbies
- Earth Sciences
- Education
- Ephemera
- Fiction
- Folklore
- Geography
- Health & Diet
- History
- Hobbies & Leisure
- Humor
- Illustrated Books
- Language & Culture
- Law
- Life Sciences
- Literature
- Medicine & Pharmacy
- Metaphysical
- Music
- Mystery & Crime
- Mythology
- Natural History
- Outdoor & Nature
- Philosophy
- Poetry
- Political Science
- Science
- Psychiatry & Psychology
- Reference
- Religion & Spiritualism
- Rhetoric
- Sacred Books
- Science Fiction
- Science & Technology
- Self-Help
- Social Sciences
- Symbolism
- Theatre & Drama
- Theology
- Travel & Explorations
- War & Military
- Women
- Yoga

We kindly invite you to view our extensive catalog list at:
http://www.kessinger.net

This Volume Is
AFFECTIONATELY DEDICATED
to
MY FATHER AND MOTHER

INTRODUCTION

THE STORY of Territorial Masonry, here unfolded, is official and authoritative; it has been written by Right Worshipful Brother Ray V. Denslow, Chairman of the Masonic Service Association of Missouri, and is the contribution of that organization to the historical literature of Freemasonry.

M. W. Brother Orestes Mitchell, Grand Master of Missouri, has seen fit to give the work his approval in the following letter:

GRAND LODGE,
ANCIENT FREE AND ACCEPTED MASONS,
STATE OF MISSOURI,
March 11, 1925.

To the Masonic Fraternity of Missouri.

BRETHREN:

I know of no work being done by the Masonic Service Association of Missouri that should be more appreciated than their publication of the book on "Territorial Masonry" written by Right Worshipful Brother Ray V. Denslow.

I trust that it will be possible for every Missouri Freemason to read this volume, containing as it does, the wonderful story of the beginnings of Freemasonry in the Louisiana Purchase Territory.

Fraternally,
ORESTES MITCHELL,
Grand Master.

INTRODUCTION

It will be found to be a plain story of historical incidents, events and characters which have been recorded for the first time with the proper Masonic background.

CONTENTS

CHAPTER		PAGE
I	THE LOUISIANA TERRITORY	1
II	FREEMASONRY OF THE TERRITORY	8
III	MASONIC PATHFINDERS	18
IV	MASONIC PIONEERS	34
V	POLITICAL AND MILITARY LEADERS	62
VI	MASONIC DUELISTS	75
VII	THE MOTHER LODGE OF THE MISSISSIPPI VALLEY	94
VIII	THE STORY OF LOUISIANA LODGE No. 109	117
IX	THE LODGE OF MERIWETHER LEWIS	170
X	MISSOURI'S MASONIC NEIGHBORS	196
XI	MASONRY CROSSES THE MISSOURI	209
XII	PRE-GRAND-LODGE LODGES	218
XIII	FREEMASONS AND THE STATE CONSTITUTION	230
XIV	THE FIRST GRAND LODGE IN MISSOURI TERRITORY	246
INDEX		271

TERRITORIAL MASONRY

CHAPTER I

THE LOUISIANA TERRITORY

IT HAS not been more than two centuries since a New England historian wrote: "Beyond the Connecticut River is a long line of low-lying hills—beyond which it is probable that civilization will never advance."

There may be some New Englanders who yet hold this view of the geography of the United States, but to-day, the school-child knows of the Middle West and of the wonders of the great territory once known as the Louisiana Purchase. What was once termed "Jefferson's Folly" is now the most valued of Uncle Sam's dominions, for in this district are to be found the great wheat and corn belts, and ores the value of which is almost unbelievable.

The settlement and development of this territory has been one of the most remarkable ever noted in the history of man; no section of the world's surface can furnish us with any more wonderful story than that great territory extending from the Mississippi River westward towards the Pacific Ocean. What only a few more than a hundred years ago was naught but unexplored country with a few scattering French and Spanish settlers, with here and there a roving Indian tribe, has to-day become the home of millions of citizens of the United States, containing probably more descendants of pure American blood than any other similar section.

The development of this wonderland is a story in itself, of such length and character as would be impractical and inopportune to discuss in such a volume as this. During the last few years the novelist has seized upon historical events of the earlier period of Territorial life and has brought them to the attention of the American public.

St. Louis, on the eastern outpost of this immense section, has been immortalized in a number of novels, particularly "Richard Carvel," while in the last few years thousands have been thrilled by that wonderful film production, "The Covered Wagon," taken from the novel by that name, telling the story of the "Oregon Trail," which but seventy-five years ago, was the great thoroughfare for those Pacific-bound. Many still live who can recount the trials of that period. Such scenes have been brought close to the hearts of the settlers of this great territory through family tradition and history.*

While history and romance have recorded much of this earlier life, no pen has yet attempted to show the part played by those pioneers who were members of that fraternity, whose signs and symbols unite men of every sect, country, race and opinion. True, not every pioneer was of the fraternity, but it is safe to say that of the outstanding men of the Territory, fully 85 per cent. had assumed the Mystic Tie and traveled the road which leads from the darkness of ignorance to the light of truth. The light may have been of less intensity than that furnished by the modern lodge, the path may have been a little harder to travel, but the great chain of Brotherhood forged at the rude Altar of the little lodge at the edge of the great wilderness was such as to withstand the storms and furies which lashed back and forth for more than a decade during the Morgan troubles, and which for a time even threatened to destroy the fraternity itself.

* The writer has a letter written by his great-grandfather while crossing the Oregon Trail in 1849 telling of the cholera and high water. He died of cholera a few weeks later and was buried in an unmarked grave under circumstances similar to those narrated in "The Covered Wagon."

Many a Freemason has read the story of the Lewis and Clark expedition, thrilled at the exploits of Kit Carson, admired the accomplishments of Zebulon Pike, and been entertained by the account of the visit of the Marquis de Lafayette to St. Louis. Others have marveled at the ability of Senator Thomas H. Benton and that of Edward Bates (once Attorney-General in the cabinet of Abraham Lincoln). Those who have read Mississippi Valley history will know of Pierre Chouteau, Jr., Bartholomew Berthold, the American Fur Co., General Henry Dodge and a host of other illustrious names in that galaxy of distinguished men whose foresight and ability made this country what it is to-day; yet how few know that, without exception, all of the above were active Freemasons.

The work of these men cannot be measured; it has always been true that in a new and unsettled country are hundreds who have left civilization to avoid detection for unpunished crimes; civilization's outposts have usually inherited the refuse of the human race. Those nature's noblemen, who at great sacrifice go into a new country, must be strong of heart and true to themselves to brave such conditions that their families may prosper and enjoy the fruits of their labor. Such were the men who finally triumphed over lawlessness and made the Louisiana Purchase the home of the most contented people in all the world.

It has been said that "Masonry follows the flag"; the development of the Mississippi Valley proved no exception. But it did not come with its banners flying nor drums beating, but in that silent mysterious way which has ever been its wont—through the medium of brethren whole sole desire was to spread the true gospel of fellowship and comradeship and whose only compulsory creed was a belief in the one living and true God, father of us all, who cares not what our race, our creed, our politics or our religion.

Masonry had preceded the Church (for the existing Church was not a haven for these new settlers); the result was that many were compelled to secure most of their religious solace from reading the family Bible and in attendance at the local lodge, causing many to regard the Masonic fraternity as a religion rather than a guide post to religion. As such a guide post, it bridged the gap for more than a decade and did much to cement the friendship of men of many religious faiths during a very critical period.

From the ritualistic work of our fraternity we learn:

> The greatest and best men of all ages have been encouragers and promoters of our art, and have never deemed it derogatory to their dignity to level themselves with the fraternity, extend its privileges and patronize our assemblies.

This is unequivocally true; it is demonstrated by conditions which have existed since the original purchase of the Territory, for a history of the peoples of the various states will show that those positions in the government which require ability, character and high-standing have been largely filled from the ranks of the fraternity, not because they are of the fraternity, but because the fraternity numbers such a large percentage of such men.

There has been a marvelous increase in membership since the first introduction of Freemasonry into the Louisiana Purchase. In 1804 the Freemasons west of the Mississippi might have been numbered on both hands; four years later there were two lodges in existence in the Territory, and thirteen years later a Grand Lodge was organized. The one hundred members of the fraternity who constituted the entire membership in 1820 have grown until to-day they number more than a million.

Surely the story of such a growth ought to appeal to every member of our fraternity. We have said that "Freemasonry follows the flag" and in the settlement of the Louisiana Purchase it did more than this. It helped *raise* the flag. And the story should be recorded in its full Masonic aspect, *lest some forget.*

CHAPTER II

FREEMASONRY OF THE TERRITORY

A STRANGE scene was that which ocurred on a dreary day in 1804, in front of a typical home of a well-to-do settler of that period. Looking across a broad expanse of space, dignified by the name of "street" or, as the French were wont to term it, a "rue," could be seen (gathered about a flag pole, from which hung listlessly the national standard of the great Napoleon) a small and motley gathering of inhabitants of the village of Saint Louis, then a part of the territory known as Upper Louisiana.

A closer survey would have revealed uniforms of many descriptions; here a few Spanish settlers, there a larger group of French, while scattered about might have been discovered those of English or Irish parentage. Foremost, and most active of the group, was one in the dress of a Captain of the Regular Army of the United States; he was assisted by another striking figure, apparently one of unusual intelligence and ability—he too garbed in the uniform of a U. S. Army Captain.

Slowly, but surely, the standard of the Imperial Napoleon was hauled down; those showing trace of French descent broke forth into tears, which continued until one of the assembly, inspired by the raising of the standard of the United States, which took its place, called for three cheers, which were as promptly given by a small coterie of soldiers and Americans.

The scene was the official transfer of the Louisiana Territory, March 10, 1804, from France to the United States. The one active in command was Captain Amos Stoddard, first Governor of the Territory; assisting him was Meriwether Lewis of the Lewis and Clark expedition, then awaiting the official transfer before engaging in the enterprise which was to make his name famous in the annals of discovery.

There was some excuse for tears on the part of those who felt that they were being deserted by their government in being thus transferred to a foreign power, but members of the Masonic fraternity might well have joined with loud huzza in the cheering which followed the raising of the Stars and Stripes, for the action proclaimed that, henceforth, the people of the Territory might worship God according to the dictates of their conscience; that those connected by bonds of allegiance to the mystic fraternity which unites men of many races and religions might carry on their secret rites without molestation, and that all were to enjoy the rights of free speech, free thought and free worship—rights which were to be encouraged by the advent of a great public school system.

The acquirement of the Territory by the United States, the official transfer, and its development, may well be regarded at least as semi-Masonic in character, since so many members of the fraternity are involved.

The project was the hobby of President Thomas Jefferson, claimed without any authority to be a member of the Craft; he was criticized severely by his foes, and the whole purchase was given the name of "Jefferson's Folly." But Jefferson was not of a type to be deterred very readily from a decision, and the purchase was completed, approved by Congress, and the next step was to assume control. The secretary to the President, at the time the Territory was acquired, was none other than Meriwether Lewis, who signed as a witness to the official transfer.

The Treaty of Cession was signed by Robert R. Livingston and James Monroe, representing the United States (both Master Masons, the former at one time an officer of the Grand Lodge of New York), while Barbe Marbois signed as the sole representative from France, representing the Emperor Napoleon (the latter having at one time been an initiate into the fraternity).

Laws for the new territory were enacted at Vincennes, then the capital of Indiana Territory, to which the Upper Louisiana was attached. These were framed by three judges, probably the most distinguished of whom was Henry Vanderburgh, who had received his Masonic degrees in a New York traveling lodge. He was appointed in 1797 by President Adams, a member of the Legislative Council of the Northwest Territory, and when the Council had been organized, became its President. He later was created a Territorial Judge, in which capacity he assisted in framing the laws of the Louisiana Territory; it is said that the judges had the assistance of John Rice Jones, one of the most able men of the Territory and a member of St. Louis Lodge No. 111.

The Secretary of the Territory in 1800, John Gibson, was first to receive the degree of Master Mason in Indiana Territory; he was responsible for the work of organizing the new Territory and his services were so satisfactory that he was retained in that capacity until the organization of Indiana as a State. The last Territorial Governor of Indiana was Thomas Posey (1813-16), the Grand Senior Warden of the Grand Lodge of Indiana, in 1821-22. At the election in 1816 Posey was defeated for Governor by Brother Jonathan Jennings, Indiana's first Governor; at the same time Brother Christopher Harrison was elected Lieutenant Governor.

The act of June 4, 1812, creating "Missouri Territory" was signed by the great Henry Clay, Speaker of the National House of Representatives, and later a Grand Master of Kentucky. Laws of the Territory were printed under the name "The Laws of the Territory of Louisiana," a book of 372 pages compiled by Frederick Bates, later Master of St. Louis Lodge No. 111; the book, the first to be printed in the Territory, was done in the office of Brother Joseph Charless, Sr. Bates at the time was Secretary and Acting Governor of the Territory; however, in July 1807, Governor Meriwether Lewis assumed control of the Territory; he divided the New Madrid district, creating the Arkansas district. Unfortunately, his death occurred in October 1809. Four years later another Freemason, General William Clark, accepted the Governorship, a position which he retained until Missouri became a State in 1820.

Conditions were far from ideal in the Territory, even after the United States had assumed control; Missouri was virtually a vast wilderness. Here and there between the Alleghenies and the Mississippi River were small settlements, usually along the lakes or river, while west of the Mississippi was a country practically unexplored. Except for the Lewis and Clark Expedition of 1804, the Pike Expedition of a later period and the occasional trip of venturesome fur-traders, nothing had been done towards settling the territory contained within the bounds of the Louisiana Purchase.

In the Middle West the population was sparse; hundreds of miles often intervened between settlements. Indians and marauding thieves existed by raiding these settlements and attacking those who dared to travel from town to town. Means of communication were poor; no post roads existed and travel was principally by flat boat. The population was made up of French, Spanish, negroes, Indians, and a scattering of English and Irish traders. The varied ideals of government as represented in such a diverse settlement of people could only result in dissatisfaction to all. Here were men brought up to believe in the divine right of kings, men whose very blood made them temperamentally different from others; here were men whose religion prevented them from living side by side harmoniously; here were others to whom kings and spiritual rulers were anathema; it was into this maelstrom of confusion and babel of language the Masonic fraternity had to enter to secure a foothold.

The seat of government was far distant; the people could not be made to feel a common interest in such a government; land titles created new dissensions. Into this confusion came Brother Aaron Burr, imbued with the possibilities of forming a new kingdom—sincere, but very much misguided. He failed in his mission, although enlisting many adherents who later had opportunity to repent.

Lodge meetings, under such conditions, proved to be outstanding events in the lives of members of our fraternity; pioneers longed for brotherhood and companionship—that companionship which was not offered by the existing church. Protestant denominations had been proscribed by the Spanish; only occasional meetings had been held, and the Catholic church could not afford a haven of refuge for the heretic Freemasons, against whom the papal thunder had been launched just a few years previously.

How remarkable, in view of such conditions, that Freemasonry should be planted, take root, and become such a splendid plant in so few years! The foremost men of the Territory aligned themselves with the Craft, and in the language of the ritual "became encouragers and promoters of our art, never deeming it derogatory to their dignity to patronize our assemblies and extend their privileges." Whether in Wisconsin, Kentucky, Ohio, Louisiana, Indiana, Illinois or Missouri, governors, judges, merchants and professional men occupied prominent places in the councils of the Craft.

The story of Freemasonry in the Louisiana Territory is not written in the musty records of its lodges; it is not to be found in the perfunctory actions of the various Grand Lodges nor in the traditions of our fraternity, which have been handed down from generation to generation. The essayist Pope gave us the answer to our question, when he uttered the statement

"The proper study of mankind is man."

We shall therefore study the foundations of Freemasonry in the Territory by resorting to an analysis of the men who composed the first lodges, who were responsible for the introduction of the fraternity into our territory, and who formed the first Grand Lodge of Missouri. Such an analysis will be a cross section of the body politic; it will include rich and poor, professional and laboring men, the élite and the "hoi polloi," men of intelligence and those of little learning—and yet all of them believers in the one true God and living exponents of the doctrine of the Fatherhood of God and the Brotherhood of Man.

Even in those days the fraternity included some of whom the Craft could not feel proud; there were then, as now, those who seemed to bring nothing but discredit to the lodge which gave them Masonic birth, yet these comprised no larger proportion of the membership then than now. God has apparently ordained that we shall ever have the wicked with us—no doubt to make us appreciate the good. In our study of the personnel of these early lodges, we do not propose to use the soft stops, but rather to give both the bitter and the sweet—of which the sweet will greatly predominate.

Quite naturally Missouri occupies the place of prominence in the story—it could not be otherwise, for no lodges existed west of the Mississippi during our territorial days except Missouri lodges. The Grand Lodge of Missouri proved to be the great Masonic colonizer, granting charters to its members, which were carried over land and sea to the furthermost borders of the Fatherland; the Santa Fé and Oregon trails were dotted with members of the fraternity and at one time the Grand Lodge of

Missouri had subordinate lodges in Kansas, Nebraska, Wisconsin, Illinois, Iowa, New Mexico, Old Mexico, Utah, Washington and California. Missouri may well be called the "Mother of Grand Lodges," since the majority of Grand Lodges west of the Mississippi owe their birth to the generosity of the Grand Lodge of Missouri.

CHAPTER III

MASONIC PATHFINDERS

"FREEMASONRY follows the flag." However, the Freemasonry of territorial days did more than this—it carried the flag with it; it was represented at the transfer of the Territory in St. Louis, and from that moment its devotees assumed leadership in everything tending to develop the Territory. Freemasonry has no cause to hang its head at mention of its representatives during the years preceding statehood; they journeyed into all parts of the Great West, discovering new sources of supply, new routes, and opening up the vast wilderness for colonization.

The great fraternity had naught to sell; it did not carry the cross in one hand and the sword in the other; its purpose was then, as now, to spread the doctrine of the Brotherhood of Man, irrespective of race or religious creed, and from the history and tradition which have come down to us, we know that our early brothers were true exemplars of the tenets of our profession—Brotherly Love, Relief and Truth.

Meriwether Lewis and William Clark

FOREMOST of all Masonic pathfinders was General Meriwether Lewis, leader of the Lewis and Clark Expedition, with whom was associated General Wm. Clark. Both were honored members of the Masonic fraternity and of the same lodge—St. Louis No. 111, under charter from the Grand Lodge of Pennsylvania. Lewis had received his degrees in the old Widow's Son Lodge in Virginia, and after his return from this expedition became the first Master of St. Louis Lodge No. 111, his name appearing first on the application for Dispensation. General Clark was buried by St. Louis Lodge No. 20 with full Masonic honors.

The exploration of the Territory west of the Mississippi was the pet hobby of President Thomas Jefferson; in 1792 he proposed to the American Philosophical Society that some suitable person be secured to explore the region "by ascending the Missouri, crossing the Stony (Rocky) Mountains, and descending the nearest river to the Pacific." According to Jefferson, Captain Lewis, then stationed at Charlottesville on recruiting service, warmly solicited the execution of this purpose; he was to take with him but one man that he might not give undue alarm to the Indian tribes. Andre

Michauz, a Frenchman, was to accompany him; both set out, but were overtaken in Kentucky by orders to return.

Captain Lewis was later made private secretary to President Jefferson, who in 1803, in a confidential message to Congress, recommended the sending of an exploring party to trace the Missouri River to its source and find a satisfactory route to the Pacific. Congress approved the plan and appropriated money for the purpose. Lewis was named to head the party. President Jefferson in speaking of the choice said:

> I had now had opportunities of knowing him intimately; of courage undaunted; possessing a firmness and perseverance of purpose which nothing but impossibilities could divert from its direction; careful as a father of those committed to his charge, yet steady in the maintenance of order and discipline; intimate with the Indian character, customs and principles; habituated to the hunting life; guarded by exact observation of the vegetables and animals of his own country, against losing time in the description of objects already possessed; honest, disinterested, liberal, of sound understanding, and a fidelity to truth so scrupulous that whatever he should report would be as certain as if seen by ourselves—with all of these qualifications, as if selected and implanted by nature in one body for this express purpose, I could have no hesitation in confiding the enterprise to him.

To our Worshipful Brother, General Meriwether Lewis, was intrusted a letter of credit, signed by the President of the United States, the like of which has never been seen before or since. It is written in the President's own handwriting:

Washington, U. S. of America.
July 4, 1803.

DEAR SIR:

In the journey which you are about to undertake for the discovery of the course and source of the Missouri, and of the most convenient water communication thence to the Pacific Ocean, your party being small, it is to be expected that you will encounter considerable dangers from the Indian inhabitants; should you escape those dangers, and reach the Pacific Ocean, you may find it imprudent to hazard a return the same way, and be forced to seek a passage round by sea in such vessels as you may find on the western coast; but you will be without money, without clothes and other necessaries; as a sufficient supply cannot be carried with you from hence, your resource in that case can only be the credit of the U. S. *for which purpose I hereby authorize you to draw on the Secretaries of State, of the Treasury, of War and of the Navy of the U. S.* according as you may find your draughts will be negotiable, for the purpose of obtaining money or necessaries for yourself and your men, and I solemnly pledge the faith of the United States that these draughts shall be paid punctually at the date they are made payable. . . . And to give more entire satisfaction and confidence to those who may be disposed to aid you, I, Thomas Jefferson, President of the United States of America, have written this letter of general credit for you with my own hand, and signed it with my name.

TH. JEFFERSON.

To Capt. Meriwether Lewis.

Lewis was faithful to the trust imposed in him; his party left St. Louis May 14, 1804, returning almost two years later, their mission fulfilled. Their accomplishments are set forth in all histories, and trophies of the expedition to-day occupy a prominent place in the great Jefferson Memorial Building in St. Louis.

Captain Zebulon Pike

STANDING second in the list of exploring expeditions is that of Captain Zebulon Montgomery Pike, a member of our fraternity.

There were two Pike expeditions; the first explored the sources of the Mississippi in 1805-1806, and the other, in 1806-1807, went up the Missouri and Platte Rivers, crossed the mountains and reached the Arkansas River, some of the party going down the river in canoes to New Orleans. Several other Freemasons were in the party, probably the most distinguished of whom was Dr. John H. Robinson, son of David Robinson of Western Star Lodge No. 107, at Kaskaskia; Robinson, Jr., had joined Lodge No. 13 in Virginia, later affiliating with Western Star and finally with Louisiana Lodge No. 109 at St. Genevieve, Mo. Pike and Robinson discovered Pike's

Peak and arrived in Santa Fé March 2, 1807, the advance guard of an army of Missourians who were to reach there during the next few years over the Santa Fé trail. Our story, discussing only Territorial days, will not permit us to go into the work done by such men as Kit Carson, David Waldo, Chas. Bent, Ceran St. Vrain, "Buffalo Bill" Cody, and others who did so much to open up the Great Southwest for American occupation.

Major Andrew Henry

WASHINGTON IRVING, in his book "Astoria," says, "trading posts had been established in 1808 in the Sioux country and among the Aricara and Mandan tribes; and a principal one, under Mr. Henry (Major Andrew Henry), one of the partners, at the forks of the Missouri; this Company had in its employ about two hundred and fifty men, partly American hunters and partly Creoles and Canadian voyagers."

The Andrew Henry mentioned was originally a member of the lodge at Kaskaskia, but when a lodge was organized on the Missouri side, he became one of the charter members. The old records bear witness to his wanderings, one financial report stating "absent two years and six months; dues have been remitted, $4.62." Francois Valle, formerly of No. 107, and also a charter member of Louisiana No. 109, evidently accompanied Henry on this expedition, for the same entry was made at the same time concerning him.

"Major Henry of the Mines" was born in Fayette County, Pennsylvania, about 1775, came to the Territory before the Spanish era, lived at St. Genevieve and other of the lead mining towns along the Mississippi, and was one of the first explorers to venture into the Rocky Mountains. His business must have been profitable because by 1808 he amassed sufficient capital to become a partner in the well-known Missouri Fur Co., an organization composed very largely of Freemasons. Among the partners were Pierre Chouteau, Jr., and William Clark, both members of St. Louis No. 111. An expedition sent out by this Company in 1809 carried 150 well armed men and all of the partners pledged to go and remain for a specified time. They reached the Rocky Mountains at a place near Three Forks, where they found fur-bearing animals in abundance and Indians who appeared very friendly. But such good fortune was not to last; suddenly the Blackfeet began war against the newcomers, many of the trappers and many of the other men returned, leaving Henry to bear the brunt of the trouble with the Indians. He was unable to get far away from his fort, which he succeeded in holding, but he lost thirty men in so doing. By 1810 he had abandoned the fort and moved to a newer site on the north fork of Snake River, known as Henry Fork, losing more men in making the change. In 1811 Henry and his companions gave up hope and agreed to break up the party and return home as best they could, Henry probably coming down the Yellowstone.

We hear little of Henry from this time until 1822, when he associated himself with General Wm. Ashley, planning a return to Three Forks. Misfortune overtook the party on the start, one of the keel boats striking a snag on the Missouri River and sinking with a cargo valued at $10,000. This did not deter Henry, who finally reached the mouth of the Yellowstone, built a fort and spent the winter. He was again attacked by Indians, as was General Ashley, who had started out with a second party; Henry came to Ashley's relief and was ordered to return to the Yellowstone, only to be attacked again. It was while engaged in this expedition that they discovered the South Pass through the Rocky Mountains.

Henry returned to Missouri, settling in the territory south of St. Louis, between Caledonia and Potosi, and died in February, 1833.

Bartholomew Berthold, Fur Trader

IN 1798 there landed in Philadelphia a gentleman of rare culture and distinction; Bartholomew Berthold, a Tyrolean. He became naturalized at once and was soon admitted a member of the Masonic fraternity; we find him in the Mississippi Valley about 1808. Admitted as a member of Louisiana Lodge No. 109, at St. Genevieve, December 27, 1809, dimitting June 9, 1812, the records noting that he had "withdrawn and removed." At a later date we find him bearing the returns of this lodge to the Grand Lodge which met in Philadelphia.

Berthold was a business man who introduced business methods into the fur business. In 1813 we find him prominent in the organization of the first Territorial bank; in 1809 we note his advertisement as being associated with René Paul in a grocery and dry goods store in St. Louis. This was dissolved in June 1812, Berthold going into partnership the following year in a similar business with Pierre Chouteau, Jr., which interest he retained until 1817. In the meantime he married the daughter of Pierre Chouteau, Sr. The firm of Berthold and Chouteau was in reality the foundation for what later became the American Fur Co., rival of the Missouri Fur Co.; to this Masonic firm there were later added John Cabanne and Bernard Pratte, Sr., whose son Bernard, Jr., later became an officer of the Grand Lodge of Missouri. For many years the American Fur Co. monopolized the fur trade of the upper country and laid the foundation for many fortunes. Berthold died April 20, 1831.

Pierre Chouteau, the Fur Prince

NO NAME is better known in and around St. Louis than that of Pierre Chouteau, Jr., member of St. Louis Lodge No. 111; he is described as "tall of stature, erect, and of splendid proportions, his coal black hair tinged with grey in his late years, his keen penetrating black eye, his sunny countenance, his French vivacity, his voice strong, vibrating, accentuated, made an impression at once lasting and agreeable." He is said to have had no equal as a business man for nearly a half century; possessed of a genius for commerce, wise judgment and bold spirit, he acquired a reputation throughout the entire northwest which "made his name everywhere the synonym of commercial honor and personal integrity."

Chouteau was the grandson of Pierre Liguest Laclede, founder of the City of St. Louis;

Stevens says in his "History of St. Louis," that "the indomitable spirit, the grasp on immediate affairs, the keen foresight, which were traits of Laclede, the founder, descended to his grandson, Pierre Chouteau, Jr." By 1827 Pratte and Chouteau had joined forces with Astor, to which a few years later was added McKenzie, with his Columbia Fur Co. It is thought that McKenzie was a member of the Craft, although the proof is not at hand. Witness this celebrated treaty with the Assiniboine and Blackfoot Indians, arranged by McKenzie for Chouteau and his Company:

We send greeting to all mankind. Be it known unto all nations that the most ancient, most illustrious, and most numerous tribes of the redskins, lords of the soil, from the banks of the great waters unto the tops of the mountains upon which the heavens rest, have entered into a solemn league and covenant to make, preserve and cherish, a firm and lasting peace, that, so long as the water runs or the grass grows, they may hail each other as brethren and smoke the calumet in peace and friendship. On the vigil of St. Andrew, in the year 1831, the powerful and distinguished nation of the Blackfeet, Piegan and Blood Indians by their ambassadors appeared at Fort Union, near the spot where the Yellowstone River unites its current with the Missouri, and in the council chamber of the Governor, Kenneth McKenzie, and the principal chief of the Assiniboine nations, . . . conforming to all ancient customs and ceremonies, and observing the due mystical signs enjoined by the great medicine lodges, a treaty of peace and friendship was entered into by the said high contracting parties, and is testified by their hands and seals hereunto affixed, hereafter and forever to live as brethren of one large, united and happy band, and may the Great Spirit who watches over us all approve our conduct and teach us to love one another.

The Missouri Fur Co.

THE Missouri Fur Company, as organized in 1820, included the names of three Freemasons, Joshua Pilcher, Joseph Perkins and Moses B. Carson. Major Joshua Pilcher was a Virginian, a gentleman of intelligence and enterprise, Master of Missouri Lodge No. 12, under charter from the Grand Lodge of Tennessee, and a relative of Thomas F. Riddick, first Grand Master of Missouri, with whom he was associated in business for some time. In the fur trade he secured a thorough knowledge of the geography and resources of the Northwest Territory. At the death of General Clark in 1838 President Van Buren appointed him Superintendent of Indian Affairs in St. Louis, which position he filled until his death in 1843. Pilcher served as a second to Senator Thomas H. Benton in his duel with Lucas. Joseph Perkins was in St. Louis as early as 1804, having been a member of the first Grand Jury summoned at that time; he was buried by Missouri

Lodge No. 1, January 25, 1824. Moses B. Carson was a brother of the celebrated Kit Carson, and a member of the lodge at Old Franklin on the Missouri River.

The comedy which runs throughout the motion picture play, "The Covered Wagon," has its origin in one of the expeditions of Andrew Henry. James Bridger, a St. Louis product, joined the Henry expedition of 1822; he was a real trapper with a wonderful sense of direction. He was never lost in the wilds and disliked the cities. He married a Shoshone wife. Bridger is the original of the character furnishing the comedy in the play; some of the scenes are adapted from incidents which occurred on the trip in which Bridger had no small part. Two members of the party were expert riflemen who could shoot a cup of whiskey from the other's head at seventy yards. One of the last exploits of this happy-go-lucky party was to shoot the heel off a negro who had a protruding heel; the pleasantry came very near delaying the party as the law took a hand in the matter.

John Hay

JOHN HAY, SR., was the last British Governor of Upper Canada; dying in 1785, his son John, Jr., was thrown upon his own resources at the age of seventeen. Through the influence of friends he was fitted out with an equipment and set out from Montreal for the Northwest; by "equipment" is meant supplies of guns, blankets, flints, powder, knives, etc., for trading with the Indians. Starting in a birch-bark canoe, he made for the base of the Rockies; he returned from this expedition with a sole Indian companion, whom he dismissed on their arrival at Prairie du Chien. Hay came on to Cahokia in 1793, where he engaged in business, later filling many public offices. He was listed as a charter member of Missouri No. 1, coming from Western Star No. 107.

One of the first settlers of the old town of Cahokia, on the Illinois side of the Mississippi River, was one John Hays, who while yet a youth engaged in the fur trade up and down the Mississippi. Possessed of likable character, he gradually built up a good business, and his boats made annual trips to Prairie du Chien as well as other upper Mississippi River points. He became Postmaster at Cahokia, a position which he held until the State was organized; he also served as sheriff of St. Clair County, and in 1822 was made Indian agent of the Potawatamis and Miamis at Ft. Wayne in Indiana. He lived to a ripe old age and died respected by all who knew him; he received his Masonic degrees in the old lodge at Kaskaskia, Ill., during February and March 1806, on the same dates as did John Hay.

General Henry Dodge

BEST known of all the members of Louisiana Lodge No. 109 was undoubtedly General Henry Dodge, who by his own exertions rose from common surroundings until he sat in the United States Senate at Washington, representing the State of Wisconsin.

Dodge was initiated in Western Star Lodge No. 109 at Kaskaskia, Ill., December 6, 1806, receiving his other degrees the following year, and in 1807 petitioning, together with other residents of St. Genevieve, for a charter from the Grand Lodge of Pennsylvania. He later served as Master of his lodge (No. 109) and at the institution of Unity Lodge No. 6, Jackson, Mo., we find him acting as installing officer.

St. Genevieve was not at any time celebrated for its moral atmosphere, but Dodge was a young man with ambition, not easily influenced; his education was truly received in the University of Hard Knocks. He was intended for a military life; in the war of 1812 he was engaged all of the time in defending the frontier; he had previous to our entering the war been made General of the Missouri militia. Having been placed in command of four hundred men, he succeeded in removing the Miami Indians (without giving offense), to a place on the Wabash River, lest they might be too easily influenced by other hostile tribes. He became the first United States Marshal in Missouri on the organization of the State, but in 1822, emigrated to Michigan Territory.

One of the greatest services rendered his government was during the Black Hawk War; Dodge proved to be a most able defender of the frontier, organizing all male persons for the defense of their firesides. He acquired quite a reputation during this campaign, and at its close was made Colonel of a regiment of dragoons; in 1833 he marched at the head of this regiment across the plains to the Rocky Mountains, making treaties with many tribes, and returning with his regiment intact. He became Governor of Wisconsin Territory and Superintendent of Indian affairs, serving with distinction.

CHAPTER IV

MASONIC PIONEERS

THE Freemasons who came to Louisiana Territory in the period 1804-20 were neither princes nor paupers; the ranks of the fraternity have always been filled from the men of the great middle class: doctors, lawyers, ministers, teachers, and those professions which create the social, religious, economic, and educational life of a community. These brothers came here for the primary purpose of making a living; they asked but a decent wage for their daily toil. The ideals of these Master Masons were high. Were their ideals higher than those of to-day? We can only surmise.

The functions of the physician have always been the same. Our medical brother of 1804 knew but little of the modern theories; Roentgen rays, analysis and hygiene were not of his time; he was not concerned with American Medical Societies, Masseurs, Chiropractics, Osteopaths, Mental Healing or Science; he had a field entirely his own. No signs on our ancient brothers' door of "10 to 12" and "2 to 4";

his door was always open to the cry of sickness and danger, whether in the plantation home of the planter or the rude hut of the backwoodsman. No closed limousine with chauffeur in livery; no paved streets with electric lights; and no steel or concrete bridges to assist in spanning the tide; instead, he journeyed on foot, or by horse, over rough trails and across swollen streams. Probably the patient was too poor to ever reimburse him for his night of trial, but what should he care, whose mission was to minister unto his neighbor and restore him to health, to the end that some day he might repay by labor, by provisions or by money, the service performed by his friend and neighbor, the Territorial physician?

The First American Physician

THE honor of being the first American physician west of the Mississippi, undoubtedly belongs to Brother Aaron Elliott, well-known Master of Louisiana Lodge No. 109, who came to this country even before it came into the possession of the United States and settled near St. Genevieve. He came to Missouri from Connecticut, where he undoubtedly received his Masonic degrees, for we find him a visitor at Kaskaskia (107) December 27, 1806, the Feast of St. John the Evangelist, a Masonic ceremony at that time religiously observed. He next appears as one of the signers of the application for a dispensation for Louisiana Lodge, being recommended in the petition as Master of the new lodge. The annual returns of the lodge, which carried him as a Past Master, note his death in July 1811. Elliott and his family were deservedly popular among the people of St. Genevieve; one of his daughters married William C. Carr, later of St. Louis, while the other married Leon DeLassus, son of Camille DeLassus of the old Spanish families.

Senator Lewis Linn

ST. GENEVIEVE was the home of another physician even better known than was Brother Elliott; this was Lewis F. Linn, half-brother of Hon. Henry Dodge and later United States Senator from Missouri. Linn began to practice in St. Genevieve about 1815. The story of Senator Linn appears in almost every Missouri text book and will not here be repeated; following his death his colleague in the Senate, Hon. Thomas H. Benton, delivered a wonderful eulogy which appears in his "Thirty Years in the U. S. Senate." Linn received Masonic light in Louisiana Lodge No.

109, somewhere between 1815-24, according to a letter written by Henry Keil, once Master of the lodge.

Other Pioneer Physicians

IN THE Cape Girardeau district Brother Thomas Neale, of Virginia, practiced medicine. At Jackson, Mo., in 1816, he signed the application for Lodge Unity No. 6. Dr. Neale is credited with being in the Territory in 1805.

Two celebrated characters of the period were the two brothers, both doctors, Walter and Ezekiel Fenwick and both Master Masons. We shall learn more of these brothers in the Chapter on "Masonic Duelists." They were Kentuckians, sons of a Thomas Fenwick, and came to Missouri about 1797. Dr. Walter Fenwick was born in 1775, marrying in 1801 Miss Julie Valle, a daughter of Don Francesco Valle, member of a very prominent family. He was initiated a member of Western Star Lodge No. 109 at Kaskaskia in 1806, but did not receive his third degree until November 30, 1808, and took his dimit the same evening, evidently with the notion of joining another lodge. His death in the duel of October 1, 1811, ended his career. The brother, Ezekiel, "kept a house of entertainment" (hotel) opposite old Wittenburg for many years; he received his degrees in Louisiana Lodge No. 109, and from the evidence we are led to believe the fraternity profited as much as he when he dimitted November 13, 1809.

At Jackson, Mo., another physician, Dr. Edward S. Gannt, was one of the signers of the by-laws of Unity Lodge No. 6, Jackson, Mo. (1820). He was an attendant at Grand Lodge on the occasion of the making of Lafayette the first honorary member. It is said that he came here immediately following the War of 1812, having served as a physician during that war; he was the father of three beautiful daughters, one of whom married Brother Jonathan Guest, and another, Dr. Arthur Nelson. The newspaper in St. Louis carried the following advertisement of our brother, November 1, 1816, it having been considered "ethical" at that time to advertise:

> Doct. Ed. S. Gannt.
> Offers his professional services to the
> citizens of St. Louis and vicinity at
> the house lately occupied by
> Mad'e Lebeau, South Main St.

Among the first physicians settling near the Old Franklin settlement was Dr. Hardage Lane, a member of the Second Territorial Legislature of 1815, and the Third Territorial Legislature of 1816. He was a member of Franklin Union Lodge No. 7, of almost forgotten fame; he represented his lodge in several communications of the Grand Lodge and in 1826-7 was made Deputy Grand Master. During 1828, 1829, and 1830 he presided over the Craft as Grand Master. He is recorded as a visitor at Missouri Lodge No. 1, April 3, 1831, and at Missouri Royal Arch Chapter, August 13, 1827, the roster showing his membership to be in Vincennes (Ind.) Chapter No. 1. His wife was Ann Rebecca Carroll, daughter of Charles Carroll, killed in the Gentry duel.

Dr. Bernard G. Farrar, according to Brother Fred Billon, was the earliest of the physicians in St. Louis Territory; he was a member of Hiram Lodge No. 4, in the State of Kentucky, his name being in the list (1808) of suspensions for non-payment of dues. He later paid up his dues and affiliated with the lodge at St. Louis (No. 111). He arrived in St. Louis in 1807; originally a Virginian, coming from the same country as did Edward and Frederick Bates, he settled in Kentucky, near Frankfort, where he practiced medicine for some time. A brother-in-law, Judge Coburn, having received the appointment as judge of the Louisiana Territory, he was encouraged to move farther west. He came to St. Louis and formed a partnership with Dr. David V. Walker. Brother Farrar acted as surgeon in the Benton-Lucas duel. His first wife was Sarah Christy, daughter of Brother Wm. Christy. He was born July 4, 1785 and died in 1849.

Dr. Samuel G. J. DeCamp came to this country about 1819 and practiced in St. Louis; he is listed as one of the visitors who attended the preliminary convention for the organization of the Grand Lodge of Missouri.

Dr. Lewis C. Beck came to Missouri in 1819 with his brother, Abraham Beck, a lawyer; he was initiated in Missouri Lodge No. 1 in January, 1822; his brother having died, he dimitted in May of that year, returning to New York, where he published a Gazeteer and other books dealing with the States of Illinois and Missouri.

Dr. John H. Robinson

ONE of the most noted of all, however, was the well-known John Hamilton Robinson, son of Brother David Robinson (Western Star No. 107) and Miriam Hamilton; he was a Virginian, born in Augusta County, January 24, 1782. His mother was a sister of the famous Alexander Hamilton. Robinson came to this country shortly after the transfer and accompanied Zebulon Pike on his expedition, as will be noted in another chapter; he was married by Auguste Chouteau, Sr., to Miss Sophie Marie Michau, December 24, 1805; he was a brother-in-law of Dr. Saugrain, credited with having brought to St. Louis in 1807 the first vaccine material. Robinson was a zealous Mason, who evidently received his degrees in Lodge No. 13, Virginia, but who later visited No. 107, and in 1811 is listed as Senior Warden of No. 111 at St. Genevieve.

First Masonic Funeral

THE first funeral recorded by Missouri Lodge No. 1, in the new burial ground at 10th and Washington Avenues, St. Louis, Mo., was that of Brother Richard Mason, who with his wife and daughters came to Missouri from Philadelphia in the year 1820; he was building a very lucrative practice at the time of his death, April 11, 1824, and his Masonic burial was largely attended by members and friends.

Some Early Lawyers

DURING the French and Spanish periods there were no courts in Upper Louisiana, the Governor of the Territory acting as judge and jury in apparently a very satisfactory manner without the aid of attorneys or lawyers. The English relinquished the Territory on the East side of the Mississippi after the War of the Revolution, but even preceding that date courts had been established in the Territory. The first lawyer known to have practiced in that Territory was Brother John Rice Jones, who had much to do with writing the first laws of Indiana Territory. In 1787 he came to Kaskaskia, where he lived for several years; at Kaskaskia was another lawyer and Mason (of whom the less said the better), Isaac Darnielle. Jones came to St. Genevieve about 1808, receiving his degrees during the months of April and May, 1815; two of his sons were Masons, one, Augustus, serving as Grand Junior Warden in 1832.

The father was active politically all of his life; he died in St. Louis, January 31, 1824, four years after participating in the State Constitutional Convention, and while a member of the Supreme Court of Missouri. One daughter became the wife of Brother Thomas Brady, of Missouri No. 12; another became the wife of Brother (Hon.) John Scott. Jones was a splendid citizen, a Welshman, born February 10, 1759; he was with George Rogers Clark at the capture of Vincennes; it is recorded of him that he was "a man of indefatigable industry, extensive experience and tact for business, in private life a friend of the indigent, the ignorant and distressed, who found in him a benefactor; he had an active mind, constantly engaged; was a living chronicle of passing events, and a student until the day of his death; a correct judge of passing events and knew much of men and things."

Senator John Scott

ONE of the charter members of Louisiana Lodge No. 109, and later its Master, was the Honorable John Scott, a son-in-law of Brother John Rice Jones. Scott, a native Virginian and graduate of Princeton College, arrived in 1804, stopping for a time at Vincennes, where he was admitted to the bar, and in 1805 opening up a practice in St. Genevieve. He was elected to the first Territorial Legislature, then as Territorial Delegate to Congress, and became the first Representative in Congress following Missouri's admission as a state. His vote for Adams in the Presidential race between Adams and Missouri's favorite, Andrew Jackson, cost him his seat in Congress. Scott's honesty and integrity were always above reproach and he held the confidence of the people. He died at the extreme age of 80 years. His name is perpetuated in the naming of Scott County, Missouri. We shall again refer to him in a later chapter.

Alexander Buckner

IN THE City of Cape Girardeau, Mo., there stands a monument of marble, resting on a granite pedestal; on the top of the stone is the Holy Bible with the square and compasses; on its face is the inscription:

> Alexander Buckner
>
> Born in Kentucky in 1785
> Died in Missouri, June 6, 1833.
>
> President of the Convention, and
> *First Grand Master* of the
>
> *State of Indiana*
>
> Elected and installed January 12, 1818.
>
> United States Senator from Missouri at the time of his death.
>
> Erected by the Grand Lodge,
> F. & A. Masons of the State of Indiana.
> A.D. 1897, A.L. 5897.

Brother Buckner was born in 1785 in Kentucky; in 1812 we find him in Indiana engaged in the law business. He appeared at the preliminary convention for the organization of the Grand Lodge of Indiana, representing the lodge at Charlestown, Indiana; January 13, 1818, he became the first Grand Master of Indiana; an altercation which led to the duel (discussed in another chapter) caused him to remove to Missouri about 1820, settling at Jackson, Missouri, where he built up a large practice and was regarded as one of the territory's most useful citizens. He was the leading character in the formation of Unity Lodge No. 6 (Mo.). He was circuit attorney for a time; in 1820 he was a member of the Constitutional Convention, was elected to the State Senate, and later to the House of Representatives, which position he resigned to become United States Senator for two sessions. He died in 1833.

At St. Genevieve were two other attorneys and Masons, George Bullitt and T. T. Crittenden; Bullitt received his degrees in Western Star Lodge on the Illinois side in 1806, dimitting November 7, 1807, to become a charter member of Louisiana Lodge No. 109. Bullitt represented the county in the Territorial Legislature and served as a Register of the Land Office. Crittenden was initiated in Louisiana

No. 109 in the year 1810; he was a brother of Senator J. J. Crittenden of Kentucky, but following his duel with Brother Walter Fenwick, October 1811, he was allowed to withdraw June 9, 1812, and history does not thereafter mention him.

The First Postmaster

IN Rufus Easton, first Postmaster west of the Mississippi River, Masonry had another representative citizen and lawyer. He arrived in St. Louis in 1804, one of the first members of the legal profession to settle in St. Louis; he was a member of Roman Lodge No. 82 (N. Y.) and was one of the petitioners for Western Star Charter. Later he signed as a petitioner for the dispensation of No. 111 in St. Louis, and became Junior Warden of the lodge. In 1822 he removed to St. Charles, where he died July 5, 1834, and was laid to rest in Lindenwood Cemetery. Governor Harrison appointed him prothonotary, and later Attorney General for the Territory. Easton defeated Brother Alexander McNair September 1814 in the race for delegate to Congress.

Judge Alexander Stuart

A WELL-KNOWN character was Alexander Stuart, member of St. Louis Lodge No. 111, who succeeded Brother Nathaniel Tucker as Judge of the Circuit Court in 1826. Stuart was a Virginian, born May 11, 1770; he practiced for several years at Staunton, and in Campbell County, Virginia, later removing to Richmond, where he served on the Executive Council. Receiving an appointment as Territorial Judge of the new Territory of Illinois, he took up residence for a time in Kaskaskia, Illinois. He came to St. Louis in 1808 and acquired a wide acquaintance with the leading men of the day. Before departing on his fatal trip to Washington, D. C., General Meriwether Lewis appointed Brother Stuart together with two other brethren to act as his attorneys. Stuart died in December, 1832 while visiting relatives in Virginia.

Nathaniel B. Tucker

IN Nathaniel Beverly Tucker Missouri possessed a remarkable citizen, and the Masonic fraternity an outstanding member; he became one of the most representative Grand Masters the fraternity of Missouri has ever had. A polished gentleman with a classical education and wonderful ability, made him one of the most unusual citizens of his period. He, like many of his associates, was a Virginian, born in Williamsburg, September 6, 1784, a son of St. George Tucker of that State. He graduated from William and Mary College in 1801, studied law and practiced in Virginia until 1815, when he came to Missouri. He was a member of Missouri Lodge No. 1, and second of Grand Masters, serving three terms. Brother Tucker has often been termed "eccentric." On his arrival in Missouri he purchased a farm near Florissant, and, having hollowed out a large sycamore tree some ten feet in diameter, he set up his law office therein, cutting the top of the tree off about ten feet above ground, laying a floor, making a window opening and arranging his law books around the sides of his improvised office. He later returned to Virginia, where he died August 26, 1851.

William C. Carr

BROTHER William C. Carr was another Virginia lawyer who came to Missouri to practice his profession; he was a son of Walter Carr of Albemarle County, Virginia, noted for his friendship with Thomas Jefferson. From his birth, April 15, 1783, he was given all the advantages of the time in the matter of education. After having been admitted to the bar he came to St. Louis, the new Eldorado, in March 1801, his manner of transportation being a keel boat. He decided to practice in St. Genevieve, but remained there but a year, returning to St. Louis; while in St. Genevieve he married the daughter of Brother (Dr.) Aaron Elliott. He became circuit judge and was an influential man in many ways. His first wife having died, he married the daughter of Brother Silas Bent; his death occurred March 31, 1851. He was a member of Meriwether Lewis' Lodge, and later Missouri No. 12.

Silas Bent

JUDGE Silas Bent deserves mention here as one of the pioneers in the legal profession. A Massachusetts man of distinguished ancestry (born 1768), he came at twenty years of age to Ohio, where he remained until 1806, when he took up residence in St. Louis. Friendship having secured him appointment as Deputy Surveyor of the Territory in 1807, he became judge of the Court of Common Pleas and Quarter Sessions. Later he was Clerk of the County Court and Recorder, his death occurring in 1827. He was a member of Missouri Lodge No. 12, and his son, Governor Charles Bent, a member of Missouri No. 1.

Henry S. Geyer

CAPTAIN Henry S. Geyer was a member of Missouri Lodge No. 12, noted for having defeated Thomas H. Benton in the race for the United States Senate. He was born in Frederick County, Maryland, December 9, 1790. Studying law under the tutelage of an uncle, he was in the War of 1812 as a Paymaster. He came to St. Louis in 1815 and opened up a law practice. In 1817 he compiled a Digest of the Laws of the Territory. He became, successively, member of the Territorial Legislature, first Speaker of the House of Representatives (1821), member to the Committee on Revision of State Laws (1824) and U. S. Senator (1851). His second wife was a daughter of Brother Rufus Easton. He died March 5, 1859. While a great jurist, Brother Geyer is best known for his argument in the celebrated Dred Scott case, much of his reasoning being cited in the opinion of Chief Justice Taney.

Ezra Hunt

IN THE northwestern part of Missouri, near Louisiana, lived Judge Ezra Hunt, who signed the application addressed to the Grand Lodge of Tennessee in 1821 asking for a dispensation for a lodge at Louisiana, Mo., which later resulted in his being made Master of Harmony Lodge No. 4. Hunt appeared at several sessions of the Grand Lodge and became an excellent Masonic worker; it is not known where he received his degrees, but it was probably in Tennessee, where he taught school for a year following his graduation at Harvard College in 1816. He was admitted to the bar in 1819, and died in 1860, an influential and highly respected citizen.

John F. Ryland

PAST GRAND Master John F. Ryland settled in central Missouri in 1819 for the purpose of practicing law. He, too, was a Virginian, born in King and Queen County in 1797. He came to Kentucky with his father in 1809, and was educated at Forest Hall Academy, later opening a private school, and at the same time studying law under Judge Hardin. He first made his home in old Franklin, where he was a member of Franklin Union Lodge No. 7, but later moved to Lexington, where he lived until his death in 1879. He is said to have been one of the first of his profession to practice south of the river. He became Circuit Judge, and in 1848, Judge of the Supreme Court. History records him as one of the outstanding jurists of the time. His son, Xenophon Ryland, also became Grand Master of Missouri.

Governor H. R. Gamble

HAMILTON ROWAN GAMBLE practiced in Franklin, although he spent some time in St. Louis; Governor Frederick Bates in 1824 appointed him Secretary of State and he became a resident of St. Charles. In 1851 he became Judge of the Supreme Court and in 1861 Governor of Missouri at a time when it required men of wisdom and personality to hold the government intact. Gamble took an important part in the history of the Grand Lodge, becoming Grand Master in 1832.

Other Lawyers

ANOTHER lawyer in the Territory was Judge Robert Wash, born in Virginia in

1790 and educated at William and Mary College. He served on the staff of General Howard during the Indian campaign of the War of 1812. President Monroe appointed him United States Attorney and from 1824-37 he was a judge of the Supreme Court of Missouri. He was a member of Missouri No. 1, and was one of those in attendance on the occasion of the Grand Lodge session held for General Lafayette.

Colonel Robert P. Farris was a member of Missouri Lodge No. 1; he was born in Natick, Mass., in 1794 and came to St. Louis about 1815; we find him in 1820 in command as Lieutenant Colonel of the first regiment of militia and in 1822 he became Colonel. Governor McNair appointed him Circuit Attorney for St. Louis. He married at Potosi, Missouri, a daughter of Captain (and Brother) Joseph Cross, referred to in the History of St. Louis Lodge No. 111.

Archibald Gamble, brother of Hamilton R. Gamble, was an attorney in St. Louis from 1816 on; he was a native Virginian, married a daughter of Brother Rufus Easton, and became attorney for the St. Louis public schools. He was very active Masonically, a member of the St. Louis Lodges, and prominent in the reception of General Lafayette in 1825.

Brother A. L. Magennis, member of Missouri Lodge No. 1, was listed as an attorney in St. Louis as early as 1818.

Other members of the Cooper County bar were William J. Redd and Hamilton R. Gamble, the latter a Governor of Missouri. Here also came Major Taylor Berry, later to lose his life in the duel with Abiel Leonard. Redd, Gamble and Berry were all members of the Craft. Berry was a Paymaster during the War of 1812, and distinguished himself by saving the funds of the army at the surrender of Detroit. Redd was a member of Franklin Union Lodge No. 7 and an attendant at Grand Lodge.

Hon. Edward Bates

ONE WHO had great influence, recognized as without a peer in a legal way, was Edward Bates, member of Missouri Lodge No. 12 (later Missouri No. 1) and Grand Master in 1825-26-27-31. Bates was born in Belmont, Virginia, of Quaker parents September 4, 1793. His brother, Frederick, being Secretary of the Territory, he came to St. Louis in 1814 to make his home with him and to study law in the office of Brother Rufus Easton. He was admitted to the bar in 1816, and rapidly rose to the front rank of his profession. His work in the formation of the Grand Lodge of Missouri, and that having to do with the State Constitution will be discussed in other chapters.

In 1820 he was appointed by Governor McNair as Attorney General of Missouri; in 1822 he sat in the first State Legislature assembled at St. Charles; in 1824 President Monroe recognized his ability by making him United States District Attorney for Missouri; he was the second to be elected Representative in Congress from this State, succeeding Brother John Scott. In 1830 he was State Senator; in 1834 State Representative. President Fillmore, the second President to recognize him, offered him a place as Secretary of War, which he refused. In 1853 he became judge of the St. Louis Land Court. In 1856 he presided over the Baltimore Convention of the Whig Party, and in 1861 a third President, Abraham Lincoln, offered him the position of Attorney General of the United States. This he accepted, filling the office for two years, resigning in 1863. He died six years later at his home near St. Charles. He was a brother-in-law of another Grand Master, Hamilton R. Gamble.

Senator T. H. Benton

WE HAVE reserved for the last, one who might have been discussed in the chapter on "Masons in Politics," but since he was engaged in the practice of law at the time Missouri became a State, he is rightfully discussed here.

The nationally known Missourian, Honorable Thomas H. Benton, for thirty years met all antagonists in the arena of the United States Senate and usually emerged victorious. His "Thirty Years in the United States Senate" should be read by every public man and historian. As a public speaker and a campaigner of the old school he stood without a peer; intelligent, with an accurate knowledge of every situation and a gift of analysis, he made himself feared whenever he entered the public forum. He was turbulent, restless, egotistical and tyrannical; we have devoted considerable space to his troubles with Andrew Jackson and Charles Lucas in the chapter on "Duels." He was a charter member of Missouri Lodge No. 1, and of its predecessor, Missouri No. 12; he came to Missouri in 1813, following his trouble with Jackson. Most of his life was spent in Washington, D. C., and he rarely attended his Mother Lodge. So many text books cover the wide range of Benton's various activities we have thought it unnecessary to quote them.

In closing the section of the chapter dealing with lawyers who were Freemasons during the Territorial period, we note that not all of those who practiced law are mentioned, but sufficient names are given to show that members of the fraternity were amply represented in this profession.

Editors

"THE pen is mightier than the sword." In the Mississippi Valley the pen has been wielded by many members of our fraternity, and while their work may not appear on the surface, the results accomplished have been the same as that in other professions; we owe a great debt to our pioneer newspapers, for they have recorded the ambitions, the trials, the failures, and successes of the people.

First of Missouri editors was Brother Joseph Charless, who issued on July 12, 1808, the first number of the now famous "Missouri Gazette." For three years it carried the name "Louisiana Gazette" and in 1812 "Missouri Gazette and Public Advertiser." Charless was an adventurous Irishman who came to St. Louis from Louisville, Kentucky; he was usually involved in the broils of the time and found it necessary to oppose rival papers from time to time.

Brother Charless printed the first book published in the Territory, "The Laws of the Territory of Louisiana." His Masonic history is somewhat obscure; he was a member of St. Louis Lodge No. 111, and later of Missouri No. 11; he was in the lodge "limelight" on several occasions, and as a result of one of such experiences, was indefinitely suspended February 2, 1824.

In 1815 a group of those opposed to Brother Charless and some of his editorial policies organized a rival newspaper. Among the group were several Masons: Dr. B. G. Farrar, Dr. Walker, Wm. C. Carr, Robert Wash and William Christy; they raised $1,000 to start the new publication, which was to bear the title "Western Journal." Brother Joshua Norvell of Tennessee was induced to come to St. Louis to take charge of the business. But the paper was not a financial success; it was disposed of in 1817 to Brother Sergeant Hall of Cincinnati, who renamed it the "Western Emigrant," but later gave up its publication, he being unfitted for the position.

We next learn of "The Enquirer" appearing in 1819, edited by Isaac N. Henry and Evarist

Maury, the first named an active Mason. He was a member of Missouri No. 12, and represented that lodge on the only occasion it was ever represented at the Grand Lodge of Tennessee. This was the paper edited for a time by Col. Thos. H. Benton, Brother Henry having died within a short time after starting it. Brother Walter Alexander edited it for a time.

In November, 1820, Brother Minor M. Whitney of Unity Lodge No. 6 and Brother William Creath founded the "Independent Patriot" at Jackson, Missouri, which was later sold to Brother James Russell.

Ministers and Teachers

IT WAS a custom during the earlier part of the last century to employ the local minister as a teacher, since his religious duties did not demand his attention except on the one day of the week; therefore, we find many of the ministerial profession filling a dual rôle. Many of these were Freemasons.

Among the trustees of the St. Genevieve Academy were Brothers Walter Fenwick, Andrew Henry, Aaron Elliott, John Scott, Thomas Oliver, George Bullitt, Henry Dodge, and Henry Kiel; all of these were members of St. Genevieve Lodge. Brother Joseph Hertick, of the same lodge, was the leading school teacher of that section, introducing new and up-to-date methods; three of his pupils finally reached the United States Senate. Rev. Salmon Giddings, who appears to have been a Mason and a minister, taught in 1816 at St. Genevieve, having Dr. Elliott's daughter as an assistant. Mrs. Perdreauville, wife of a Master Mason, conducted an Academy in St. Louis in 1818. Elihu H. Shepherd, later an active Masonic worker, became one of the most prominent Missouri teachers. In Potosi, Missouri, Brothers John Rice Jones, Andrew Scott, and probably others, were trustees of the Academy.

Near Franklin, Howard County, Brother Grey Bynum became the first teacher and had under his instruction forty-five children at one time.

The work of Thomas F. Riddick and Joseph McFerron, John Scott and others in behalf of the public school system will be found in other chapters; needless to say, Masons of that day believed in education and were always behind any proposition having to do with the betterment of the educational facilities of the State.

In discussing Thomas F. Riddick we have mentioned the work of Rev. John Ward, first of the Episcopalian faith to enter Missouri and organize his people. He was a member of a

Kentucky lodge. Hampton Boon and Justinian Williams were both early-day ministers and very active Freemasons, both holding Grand Lodge office in Missouri. Even before their time we learn of the religious work of Rev. Josiah Dodge, one of the earliest to hold services in the Territory. It was not until after the Territory became a State that various denominations began to grow up in Missouri. Previous to that period ministers were virtually on their own resources, and were not at work as the result of any organized effort on the part of their denominations. They were, as a rule, very poorly paid, and the service they rendered to the sick, the suffering, the distressed and others could not be measured in terms of money. Their service was as real to the community as any rendered by teacher, lawyer, doctor, or editor and deserves recognition at our hands.

CHAPTER V

POLITICAL AND MILITARY LEADERS

MORE notable in many ways than the pioneer physicians, ministers and lawyers were the Freemasons who were represented in the political and military life of the great Territory.

The Territorial era was one which produced such characters as Andrew Jackson, Lewis Cass, Joseph Hamilton Daviess, Meriwether Lewis, William Clark, Henry Dodge and a score of other equally as distinguished men prominent in the annals of our fraternity. Most of those mentioned are discussed later, and we shall do no more here than to call attention to their work.

Major J. Bruff succeeded Captain Amos Stoddard as Commandant of the Upper Louisiana Territory shortly after Stoddard took over the Territory from the French. Bruff was an officer of the regular army, stationed for a time at St. Louis; he left no record of his

POLITICAL AND MILITARY LEADERS 63

previous Masonic membership, but we know him to have been one of the signers of the application for dispensation for St. Louis Lodge No. 111, as was General Meriwether Lewis. Bruff was the only one to sign as a Royal Arch Mason, making the first written record of Royal Arch Masonry in the Territory.

The government, early after acquiring the Territory, constructed a barracks and fort at Fort Bellefontaine, a short distance from St. Louis along the Missouri River. Many officers of the army, sent here from time to time, were members of the Craft, participating in the labors of St. Louis Lodge No. 111, as well as its successor, Missouri Lodge No. 1.

Practically every able-bodied man was enrolled in the Territorial militia for protection during the War of 1812 and later during Indian uprisings. Many Masons enlisted under these conditions: Colonel Thomas H. Benton, Alexander McNair, Henry Dodge, John Scott, Thomas F. Riddick, Pierre Chouteau, Jr., Nathaniel Cook, Joseph Hertick, Thomas Oliver, Stephen F. Austin, Nathaniel Simonds, John McArthur, Wm. Christy and a host of others all held commissions in the organized militia or regular army.

In 1814 General (and Brother) William Clark left St. Louis with several barges and troops for Prairie du Chien, nominally American territory, but in reality held by Indians and traders; he had as an escort 60 United States regular troops, commanded by Brother Joseph Perkins, a Lieutenant in the Army. A fort was established there and Perkins remained in charge of the post.

The defeat of the British at the Battle of New Orleans, January 8, 1815, by Brother Andrew Jackson, a General in command of the Regular Army, was a cause for great rejoicing in the Territory, many Freemasons holding commissions in his army.

As early as 1808 a meeting was held in St. Louis for the purpose of forming a volunteer company; Benjamin Wilkinson was made Captain of this first company and Risdon H. Price acted as a Lieutenant; both were members of the lodge at St. Louis. In this year General Lewis ordered all troops to be mustered according to law, at which time Brother (Capt.) Pierre Chouteau and Brother (Capt.) Otho Shrader assembled their troops of horse. Another rendezvous of these troops was held at St. Louis May 4, 1809.

A later organization, known as the "St. Louis Guards," was formed in December, 1819; we note as officers the following Master Masons: Amos J. Bruce, William Renshaw, David B.

Hoffman and Stephen Rector. Their first parade was held on Washington's Birthday, 1820.

The Battle of Tippecanoe

THE great military event of the Territorial period was the Battle of Tippecanoe, a defeat which spelled ruin for the plans of the Indian tribes of the Middle West. Early settlers in the Northwest Territory were in constant warfare with the antagonistic Indian tribes; as early as 1791 a Master Mason, General St. Clair, at the time Governor of Northwest Territory, was defeated by the Miami Indians under Little Turtle, Blue Jacket and others at a place known as Fort Washington, later the site of Fort Recovery. Brother Robert Buntin, Sr., a Captain in the War of Revolution, visiting the field three months later, gave the following pen picture of the disaster:

> I went with General Wilkinson to the field of action to recover the artillery carriages, which he was informed remained there, and to bury the dead. We arrived on the field of battle about ten o'clock the morning of February 1st. The scene was truly melancholy. In my opinion, those unfortunate men who fell into the enemies' hands were used with the greatest torture, having their limbs torn off.

In 1800 the Territory of Indiana was organized and William Henry Harrison was made Governor; the Territory did not contain more than five thousand white people, these scattered in thinly settled neighborhoods from the Ohio River on the south to the lakes on the north. Vincennes, established as a military post about 1731 and settled about the year 1735, was the capital of the Territory. The battlefield of Tippecanoe is situated in Tippecanoe County, Indiana, seven miles northeast of the present city of Lafayette, almost at the banks of the Wabash River, at a spot near which Tippecanoe Creek enters the river and near the Indian town of Prophetstown, named in honor of the brother of the celebrated Indian chief, Tecumseh.

Here in the holy city of Prophetstown the brother of Tecumseh wrought his Indian braves into a frenzy of religious ecstasy and prepared them for battle against the approaching army of General Harrison as it advanced up the Wabash River. October 3, 1811, the army encamped at Fort Harrison (present site of Terre Haute); the march was resumed and they camped at the old Indian Fort, "Ouiatenon." On November 6 the army came in view of Prophetstown; the army of less than a thousand men encamped about a mile and a half from the Indian village and endeavored to open a conference with the Indians, but without avail.

General Harrison describes the ground of his encampment in a report made following the battle:

> I found the ground destined for the encampment not altogether such as I could wish it; it was indeed, admirably calculated for the encampment of regular troops that were opposed to the regulars, but it offered great facility to the approach of savages. It was a piece of dry oak land, rising about ten feet above the level of a marshy prairie in front, towards the Prophets Town, and nearly twice that height above a similar prairie in the rear, through which and near to this bank ran a small stream clothed with willows and other brushwood. Toward the left flank this bench of land widened considerably but became gradually narrower in the opposite direction, and at the distance of one hundred and fifty yards from the right flank terminated in an abrupt point. The army encamped in the order of battle. The men were instructed to sleep with their clothes and accoutrements on, with their firearms loaded and their bayonets fixed. On the morning of the battle, November 7, 1811, I had arisen at a quarter after four, and the signal for calling out the men would have been given in two minutes, when the attack commenced. It began on the left flank, but a single gun was fired by the sentinels or by the guard in that direction, which made not the least resistance, but abandoned their officer and fled into camp, and the first notice which the troops of that flank had of the danger was from the yells of the savages within a short distance of the line.

The American troops, thus surprised, fought valiantly and succeeded in keeping the savages from their camp until daylight, when a general charge resulted in a complete rout for the Indians; the fight had been disastrous, however, for thirty-seven were found to have been killed and one hundred and fifty-one were wounded.

Foremost to fall was Colonel Joseph Hamilton Daviess, Grand Master of the Grand Lodge of Kentucky, only two months previous elected and installed by his brother Masons. On his way to the spot where he met his death he stopped at old Vincennes, and there in their lodge hall presided in the conferring of a second and third degree. As Grand Master Warren fell at Bunker Hill in defense of his country, so did Grand Master Daviess lay down his life at the Battle of Tippecanoe in defense of his country, both exemplifying in tragic manner their love for their country and their fellowman.

The Battle of Tippecanoe was won; it had accomplished the end which the American army had sought, but not without a great sacrifice of noble American men, many of whom were members of the fraternity.

In 1858 a committee from the Grand Lodge of Indiana, having secured the sword of Col. Daviess, attended the annual communication of the Grand Lodge of Kentucky and officially presented it to them, and it now rests in their archives as one of their most sacred treasures; it is contained in a box of oak made from the tree under which he received his death wound.

Other distinguished Freemasons who fell were Colonel Abraham Owen, on the staff of General Harrison as a volunteer aid. Colonel (later General) Bartholomew received serious wounds during the battle from which he never recovered; he was an intimate friend of our own Alexander Buckner and assisted in organizing the Grand Lodge of Indiana, serving as Grand Senior Warden. Two members of Vincennes Lodge were killed in the fight: Thomas Randolph, who organized the lodge, and Colonel Isaac White, on whom Daviess had conferred the second and third degrees, just previous to his departure on the expedition. Parmenas and Benjamin Beckes were two other influential Masons who accompanied General Harrison, the latter being the first white child born in the Territory. It was Major Waller Taylor, a Master Mason, who assisted in the burial of Col. Daviess and Thomas Randolph, the latter having been Attorney General of the Territory. Wm. Prince, first sheriff of the Territory and a Mason, participated in the battle, as did many others, who, while not officers, did their part and fought manfully.

Many efforts were made by the Masonic order to erect a memorial on the battlefield, but these efforts seemed to be without success; Brother John Tipton, who fought in the battle and who owned the battlefield, donated the ground to the State of Indiana, where to-day it is the Mecca for tourists from many States, the battle being a decisive one, and indirectly resulting in the election of General Harrison as President of the United States.

In taking up the study of Freemasons prominent in the political life of the territory, we necessarily trespass upon other chapters, since most of those who were prominent politically were also prominent either as military leaders, pathfinders, or as professional men.

We have called attention to the Masonic membership of the territorial Governors: General Meriwether Lewis and General William Clark; in a later chapter we shall discover the first Governor of Missouri and many of his associate officers, such as Senator Benton, John Scott, Henry Dodge, Otho Shrader, Wm. G. Pettus and a host of others were similarly connected.

A hurried survey shows in a general way the activity of members of the fraternity; the terri-

POLITICAL AND MILITARY LEADERS

tory was at first attached to Indiana Territory (1804) at which time Brother Henry Vanderburgh was one of the judges charged with making the laws for the various districts; this court established the five districts of St. Charles, St. Louis, St. Genevieve, Cape Girardeau, and New Madrid. Courts of Quarter Sessions were established and a sheriff and recorder were to be appointed for each district. Brother Otho Shrader was named as one of the judges for the Territory in 1806; at the same time Brother Frederick Bates was Secretary of the Territory.

In 1808 General Lewis and Otho Shrader were two of the three who constituted the Territorial Legislature; at this time roads were laid out from St. Louis to New Madrid and the book of Territorial Laws, compiled by Brother Bates, was printed by Brother Charless. In 1810 Brother T. T. Crittenden was made Attorney General of the Territory and in 1811 Brother William Clark was made Brigadier General of the Territorial Militia.

Three Masons were on the first Grand Jury summoned December 18, 1804. Brother Rufus Easton presented his commission as Attorney General for the district in 1805.

Brother Jeremiah Connor, mentioned as an officer of Missouri No. 12, was sheriff in 1806; he presented to the court a statement that "the jail in its present condition is insufficient to secure the safety of the prisoners confined in it, and prays the court to take such steps in the premises as the necessity of the case may require."

In 1807 Brother Wm. Christy was appointed Clerk of the Court of Quarter Sessions; the same year Judge Silas Bent presented his commission from Acting Governor Bates, appointing him first Justice of the Common Pleas. The court now consisted of the following Master Masons: Judge Silas Bent; Associates, Pierre Chouteau, Jr., and Bernard Pratte; Thomas F. Riddick, Clerk, and Jeremiah Connor, Sheriff.

On the jury for one of the first murder trials held in 1809 there were at least two Master Masons; the defendant was convicted of the murder and ordered hanged, although one of the jurors subsequently made affidavit that he did not speak or even understand the English language.

Brother Alexander McNair succeeded Jeremiah Connor as Sheriff in 1810, and Robert Wash succeeded T. T. Crittenden as Attorney General in 1811. In 1816 an act of Congress provided for a surveyor general; Brother Wm. V. Rector was appointed, and in 1817 delegated Brother Wm. G. Pettus to make a survey of St. Louis County.

In 1814 three of the four contestants for Territorial Delegate to Congress were Master Masons, McNair, Easton, and Riddick, Easton winning by a fair majority. Brother John Scott received the place in 1816 after a second election had been held.

In the Territorial Legislatures of the time the fraternity was always well represented, not only by delegates, but by those chosen as officers to carry on the work. When the last Territorial Council met, Brother Benjamin Emmons was acting as President and Brother Thomas F. Riddick as Clerk; one of its last acts was a memorial praying for State Government.

Just whether the "Erin Benevolent Society" is to be regarded as a political organization or not we cannot state. It was, no doubt, the forerunner of such societies as the Ancient Order of Hibernians, etc., which have shown touches of a political atmosphere. The E. B. S. was organized in 1818 at the home of Brother Jeremiah Connor; Brother Thomas Brady of Missouri No. 12 acted as Chairman with Brother Thomas Hanly as Secretary. Brothers Connor and Arthur Magenis were two of the committee appointed to frame resolutions; Brother Joseph Charless, Brother Hugh O'Neill and Brother Robert Ranken also participated in the organization work. Our brethren were active in many other societies which it will not be our task to discuss here.

CHAPTER VI

MASONIC DUELISTS

THE Freemason of to-day cannot understand how one who has assumed the obligations of the fraternity could engage in such a custom as dueling. Yet members of the Craft not only engaged in duels, but even challenged and fought those bound to them by the closest of fraternal ties.

It is hard to realize the peculiar code of honor which existed during the early part of the last century. No particular class was free from its effects; indeed it was more common among the "intellectuals" than any other class. Honor made strange demands in 1820!

A Grand Lodge Acts

IN many instances Masonic duels were brought to the attention of Grand Lodges, although most Grand Lodges dodged the issue in the hope that "time, patience and perseverance" might bring the solution. In Kentucky, in the year 1812, a challenge to a duel passed between two Master Masons, the challenge being borne by a third Master Mason; the bearer of the challenge was hailed before his lodge, tried and suspended for a year for a violation of the Masonic covenant, it appearing that he had made no effort to adjust their difficulties. He appealed to the Grand Lodge of Kentucky, which, following an elaborate report by a special committee, set aside the sentence of his lodge, but called the culprit before the Grand Lodge to receive censure from the Grand Master on the impropriety of his conduct. In the report the committee shuddered at the disastrous consequences which might have grown out of the challenge "yet the course pursued by Masons, heretofore, in similar cases, without incurring censure or animadversion, goes far to extenuate the offense. The frequency and multiplicity of such occurrences, unprohibited and uninvestigated, might be construed as almost tantamount to permission." The committee admitted that it was entirely improper for Master Masons to challenge or convey a challenge to a Master Mason, quoting the fundamental principle that brothers should live together in peace and harmony, but adding that it was their belief that the brother thought he was acting correctly in the matter.

The Grand Master who presided on this occasion, emboldened perhaps by this decision, was himself a principal in a duel which occurred four years later, the other principal being a *Past Master of a lodge in his home town!*

Both participants were cited to appear at the annual communication of the Grand Lodge in 1818 to answer *for having engaged in a duel.* Samuel Woodson, later Grand Master, offered the following resolution:

> That, in the opinion of this Grand Lodge, it is entirely improper and entirely repugnant to the principles of Masonry, for any of its members to engage in personal conflicts, with each other, with deadly weapons, or otherwise; and whereas, it has been signified and made known to this Grand Lodge, that a duel hath lately taken place between Grand Master ———— and Past Master ————; resolved, that they be cited to appear before this Grand Lodge at ten o'clock on Thursday next, to answer for the above departure from the principles of the Craft.

Both parties presented themselves in obedience to the summons, whereupon the Grand Lodge decided by resolution that they possessed jurisdiction in the matter. Henry Clay, well-known statesman and orator, offered a resolution appointing a committee to confer with the two defendants for the purpose of effecting a reconciliation; both Clay and Woodson were named on the committee and they speedily reported their mission successful. But this did not end the story, for another brother offered an additional resolution whereby:

> This Grand Lodge deeply deplores the unfortunate difference between M. W. Brother ———— and Past Master ———— in which they were so far unmindful of their Masonic principles and duties as mutually and deliberately to engage in a duel, thereby prostrating and sacrificing one of the great fundamentals of our Order to the false notion of honor, by which a deluded world have been too long influenced; Resolved, that it is the opinion of this Grand Lodge that the said ———— and ———— be and they are hereby expelled from all the immunities and privileges of the Order of Masonry.

The resolution was laid upon the table and the following day Henry Clay presented the following resolution, which was adopted:

> This Grand Lodge deeply deplores the unfortunate difference between ———— and ———— the unhappy combat to which it has led. This Grand Lodge cannot but condemn, in the strongest terms, that those brethren should have so far forgotten their obligations and duties as Masons, as to have engaged in such a combat; but in consideration that the said Brothers have by the intervention of this Grand Lodge, become perfectly reconciled the one to the other, and of their correct and uniformly good deportment, and that a mitigation of the punishment, which might otherwise be due, is thereby rendered expedient, therefore, Resolved, that the said Brothers ———— ————
> be suspended from the privileges of Masonry during the pleasure of this Grand Lodge.

MASONIC DUELISTS

Ten years later, in the same Grand Lodge, Brother ——————— was restored to Masonic standing after receiving a reprimand following a duel with another Master Mason a few years previous, the latter having died.

In 1808 Henry Clay himself engaged in a duel with Humphrey Marshall.

Dueling in Indiana

PARMENAS BECKES, first to receive Masonic light in the State of Indiana, and first to receive Masonic burial in that Territory, was a victim of this code of "honor." Beckes was an inn-keeper, popular, and at one time sheriff of his county; he participated in the Battle of Tippecanoe, but met his death in a duel with one Dr. Scull.

The cause of the trouble was trivial, which was true of most duels fought. Dr. Scull was reported to have stated concerning Beckes' step-daughter that "if she was as good as she is pretty, she would be a jewel." Angered by the remark, a challenge was issued and resulted in a duel fought on Illinois soil near Vincennes, in which Beckes was killed. The weapons were dueling pistols and the distance was ten paces. It is said that Scull was very reluctant to fight and at the first command fired into the air, while Beckes' aim was wild. Beckes would not consent to a reconciliation which was urged by his seconds; pistols were recharged and each assumed his position. When the command to fire was again given, both fired at the same instant. Beckes was wounded in the right side; as he dropped he exclaimed, "Doctor, you have killed me." He lived but a few moments; Scull arranged his affairs and left the country.

Duels West of the Mississippi

THE FIRST duel recorded as having occurred west of the Mississippi was that between Dr. Bernard G. Farrar and James A. Graham. Farrar was a Freemason and the first American physician to establish himself in the vicinity of St. Louis; he was a man of considerable education, having studied in Philadelphia, Lexington, Ky., and Cincinnati. Farrar was hardly to be blamed for his participation in the affair as he was, at first, merely the bearer of the challenge to Graham. Graham declined to accept the challenge, giving as his plea that the challenger "was not a gentleman." Under the code which then prevailed Farrar became the principal. The duel was fought in the year 1810 on Bloody Island, scene of many similar encounters, and Graham received severe wounds from which he never recovered, dying on his way East about a year later. His estate, consisting of a fine horse, saddle, bridle, books and clothing, was administered by Robert Wash, a member of Missouri Lodge No. 1.

Six years later, in 1816, Captain Henry S. Geyer and George Hancock Kennerly had some trifling misunderstanding; the honor code was invoked and Bloody Island in the Mississippi River again became the scene of a duel. Kennerly was wounded at the second firing; fortunately it was but a wound in the knee which crippled him for several years, and the best part of the story is that both lived to ripe old ages, became fast friends, and often recounted the folly of their younger days. Geyer is known to have been a member of the fraternity.

Others than civilians resorted to the duel as a means of settling difficulties. August 6, 1818, Captain Martin and Captain Thomas Ramsey of the First Regiment of United States Rifles met on Bloody Island, Ramsey receiving a mortal wound from which he later died. Ramsey was a visitor at Western Star Lodge No. 107 in old Kaskaskia on January 3, 1818; he was registered as a member of Cincinnati Lodge No. 13.

Captain Ramsey was buried by Missouri

Lodge No. 12 of St. Louis on August 17, 1818.

Senator Benton as a Duelist

PROBABLY the foremost and most notable of duelists was Senator Thomas Hart Benton, a member of Missouri Lodge No. 1. Benton came to Missouri from Tennessee following an altercation with the famous Andrew Jackson, later President. It does not seem from the facts given that Benton was entirely to blame; let Benton himself tell the story:

A difference which had been for some months brewing between General Jackson and myself, produced on Saturday, the 14th inst., in the town of Nashville, the most outrageous affray ever witnessed in a civilized country.

In communicating this affair to my friends and fellow-citizens, I limit myself to the statement of a few leading facts, the truth of which I am ready to establish by judicial proofs.

First, that myself and my brother, Jesse Benton, arriving in Nashville on the morning of the affray, and knowing of General Jackson's threats, went and took our lodgings in a different house from the one in which he stayed, on purpose to avoid him.

Second, that the General and some of his friends came to the house where we had put up, and commenced the attack by leveling a pistol at me, when I had no weapon drawn, and advancing upon me at a quick pace, without giving me time to draw one.

Third, that seeing this, my brother fired upon General Jackson when he had got within eight or ten feet of me.

Fourth, that four other pistols were fired in quick succession, one by General Jackson at me, two by me at the General, and one by Col. Coffee at me. In the course of this firing General Jackson was brought to the ground, but I received no hurt.

Fifth, that daggers were drawn; Col. Coffee and Alexander Donaldson made at me and gave me five slight wounds.

Sixth, my own and my brother's pistols carried two balls each; for it was our intention, if driven to our arms, to have no child's play. The pistols fired at me were so near, that the blaze of the muzzle of one of them burnt the sleeve of my coat, and the other aimed at my head at little more than arm's length from it.

Seventh, Capt. Carroll was to have taken part in the affray, but was absent by permission of General Jackson, as he has since proved by the General's certificate—a certificate which reflects I know not whether less honor upon the General or upon the Captain.

Eighth, that this attack was made upon me in the house where the Judge of the District, Mr. Searcy, had his lodgings. So little are the laws and its ministers respected. Nor has the civil authority yet taken cognizance of this horrible outrage.

These facts are sufficient to fix the public opinion. For my own part I think it scandalous that such things should take place at any time, but particularly so at the present time, when the public service requires the aid of all its citizens. As for the name of *courage,* God forbid that I should ever attempt to gain it by becoming a bully.

Those who know me know full well that I would give a thousand times more for the reputation of Croghan in defending his post, than I would for the reputation of all the duelists and gladiators that ever appeared on the face of the earth.

THOMAS HART BENTON,
Lt. Col. 39th Inft.

Franklin, Tenn.
September 10, 1813.

Benton later became reconciled with his friend, Andrew Jackson, and Jackson had no stauncher supporter than Benton proved to be on the floor of the United States Senate in later years.

The one dark spot in Benton's life was his duel with Charles Lucas. Be it said to the credit of the distinguished Missourian, he was not the one who issued the challenge, yet it was his overbearing way which brought on the trouble.

Lucas himself prepared the statement of fact, which does not seem to have been disputed by Benton. Lucas issued his statement on the evening of August 11, 1817, preceding the duel:

> At the election held on the 4th of August, 1817, when Benton offered his vote, Lucas inquired if he, Benton, had paid the tax in time to enable him to vote—Benton then applied abusive and ungentlemanly language to Lucas, and Lucas then challenged him.

On the morning of August 12, 1817, they met and fired one round, Lucas receiving a wound in the neck and Benton one below the knee. Lucas was too badly wounded to continue and assured Benton's second that he was satisfied. Benton, hearing the reply, informed them that *he* was not satisfied and demanded a second meeting; friends attempted to adjust matters, and for a time it appeared that all was well, but within ten days following the amicable adjustment, Benton issued a second challenge "alleging that friends of Lucas had circulated statements derogatory to him, Benton." The day following the receipt of the challenge both parties met on an island above St. Louis, took the regulation ten paces distance, and fired. Benton was unharmed, but his ball went through the right arm of Lucas, penetrating his body, so that he expired in an hour. Lucas was but twenty-five years of age and the sympathy of the community was with his family. His father remained a bitter enemy of Benton until his death.

Benton later realized the uselessness of dueling and took every opportunity to speak against it, going so far as to propose laws against such a custom; by the time of his death the custom had ceased throughout the United States, general opinion backed by stringent laws compelling men to secure their revenge in other ways.

A Grand Master Duelist

UNITED STATES Senator Andrew Buckner, first Master of Unity Lodge No. 6, of Jackson, Mo., was another who engaged in a duel; the circumstances came to the attention of the Grand Lodge of Indiana since Buckner was at the time Grand Master, in fact the first of Indiana Grand Masters. His opponent was Col. Thos. H. Blake, prominent in political and military circles of the Territory. The only facts known are incorporated in the report of the committee appointed by Vincennes Lodge No. 1, Vincennes, Ind.

We, the undersigned committee appointed to inquire into the Masonic conduct of Brothers Thos. H. Blake and Alexander Buckner, report as follows; That on or about the 15th of July, 1818, in the town of Liverpool, in the County of Daviess, State of Indiana, a common assault and battery did take place between Brothers Blake and Buckner, and each did strike and seize the other. That a few days after said fight, at the town of Vincennes, a challenge to fight a duel was sent by Brother Blake to Brother Buckner, and by him accepted, and that a day or two after such acceptance said Brothers did meet in the County of Crawford, Territory of Illinois, and there did exchange a fire and fight a duel. For testimony to support this report, your committee refer to the following brothers: Robert Sturgis, General W. Johnson, Jonathan Doty and George R. C. Sullivan.

The report was received by the lodge, but no action was ever taken in the matter, Buckner removing in a few months to Missouri, settling near the town of Jackson, where he became a leading citizen and finally United States Senator, dying a natural death in 1833.

The Duel of Illinois' First Governor

IN 1790 there came to the town of Kaskaskia, Indiana Territory, one John Rice Jones, the first lawyer in the State of Illinois. Jones was an influential member of the Masonic fraternity and highly respected by all who knew him; when his oldest son was born in 1781, he was given the name, "Rice Jones." The son was a second edition of the father; he received a splendid education, for the times, in medicine and law, and came to Kaskaskia in 1806 where he opened a law office. Possessed of strong intellect, excellent education, of a prominent family, and with considerable ambition, prospects were flattering for a wonderful future. Then politics entered his life; he took to the political stump and became a zealous partisan. Although young, he had been made representative in the Indiana Territorial Legislature, and was regarded as a party leader. Only those who lived during the time can understand how easy it was for such an atmosphere to breed a quarrel. A controversy broke out between young Jones and Shadrach Bond, Governor-elect of the State of Illinois, and a duel was arranged for an island in the Mississippi River between Kaskaskia and St. Genevieve.

Both parties took their places and were about to fire; Jones' pistol, having a hair trigger, went off before the command of fire. Under the code, this gave to Bond the right to fire at Jones, but Bond, according to historians, "with that greatness of soul that appeared in all of his actions, public and private, cried out, 'It was an accident.'" The parties settled the dispute on the ground. A quarrel ensued between Jones and Dunlap, Bond's second, resulting in Dunlap shooting Jones on the streets of Kaskaskia. Dunlap escaped to Texas and was never apprehended. John Rice Jones, Sr., was a Freemason, as was Shadrach Bond, who later became the first Grand Master of the Grand Lodge of Illinois. Dunlap is probably the Dr. James Dunlap, formerly of St. Paul's Lodge No. 54, N. Y., carried on the records of Western Star Lodge No. 107, and expelled in 1813.

The Crittenden-Fenwick Duel

DR. WALTER FENWICK, a member of Western Star Lodge No. 107, engaged in a duel in 1810 with the lawyer, Thomas T. Crittenden of the same County, and a member of the same lodge. The affair was brought on by a criticism of one Ezekiel Fenwick (also a member of Louisiana Lodge), brother of Dr. Walter Fenwick, by Lawyer Crittenden in a lawsuit; Ezekiel, incensed at the tirade, induced his brother, the Doctor, to bear a challenge to a duel. Crittenden refused to meet Ezekiel in duel, whereupon Dr. Walter Fenwick, regarding the refusal (he had stated he did not regard the challenger as a gentleman) as a personal affront to the family, himself challenged Crittenden. The affair was held on Moreau's Island in the Mississippi, near St. Genevieve, Fenwick falling at the first fire while his antagonist was unharmed. Fenwick is said to have been an "eminent physician and a polished gentleman." It is to be noted that both seconds were members of Louisiana Lodge, and were distinguished men of the time, one General Henry Dodge, the other Hon. John Scott, later U. S. Senator.

An Original Bad Man

THE original bad man of Missouri was the famous John Smith, T. His name is recorded as a member of Louisiana Lodge No. 109. In 1819 Lionel Browne, nephew of Aaron Burr, and a lawyer at Potosi, Mo., challenged John Smith, T., and a duel was fought near Herculaneum; Augustus Jones, son of John Rice Jones (whose son was slain in a duel) was Browne's second; Jones was a member of a Missouri Lodge. Col. McClanahan was Smith's second. Browne was shot in the center of the forehead and died instantly.

Smith was an unusual character in an age of remarkable characters. He has been described as "judge and desperado, native of Georgia and emigrant from Tennessee." By the addition of the letter "T" he sought to distinguish himself from a large number of other Smiths. The "T," according to his reasoning, denoted the State from which he came, "Tennessee." Smith reached Upper Louisiana in 1800, his home being at Shiboleth, in the St. Genevieve district. He prided himself on his armory and is reputed to have kept two colored men busily engaged in manufacturing guns, which had the reputation of being the best made in the Territory. He was tall, of slight stature, wiry, mild-mannered, courteous except when aroused, and his skill and daring were known throughout this section.

When Aaron Burr set out to invade Mexico, he visited St. Genevieve and interested Smith, T., and General Henry Dodge in his plans; they even went so far as to go to New Madrid to join the expedition; learning of the President's proclamation, they quit the expedition and returned to St. Genevieve, where they were arrested for having enlisted in such a campaign, and it was only after they had proved the sincerity of their intentions that they were released from custody.

Smith once visited Washington to represent the interests of the people of the Territory in pending legislation. He made one trip to Chihuahua, Old Mexico, in an attempt to overturn their government, and in 1806 he became a Territorial judge. Having shot a man, he was defended by the Hon. John Scott, who succeeded in acquitting him. When the historian, Breckenridge, visited him and was entertained by him, Smith presented him with a brace of pistols guaranteed never to miss fire. Breckenridge tells of having seen him invade a bear's den in the rocks, crawling in on belly, torch in hand, and shooting him, lying down so that the bear might rush out over his body.

McFerron-Ogle Duel

ONE of the first duels after the transfer of the Territory took place between Joseph McFerron, a member of Western Star Lodge No. 107, and William Ogle; it was fought in 1807 in Cape Girardeau. It appears that Ogle insulted McFerron, struck him in the face, and finally challenged him to a duel. Although McFerron had never fired a gun, he accepted. They met on a sand bar, known as Cypress Island, and Ogle fell at the first shot. McFerron resigned his public office, but he had public sympathy with him and was later reinstated in his position. McFerron was a member of the State Convention of 1820, and later affiliated with a Missouri lodge.

A Fitting Climax

AN amusing story is related in the Missouri Historical Review of a duel in which Hon. Hamilton H. Gamble, later to be Governor of Missouri and Grand Master of the Grand Lodge of Missouri, was slated to be a second.

While Gamble, Abiel Leonard and John R. French were "young limbs of the law" at Old Franklin, Mo., French and some one whose name is forgotten, agreed to fight a duel. Gamble and Leonard were the seconds. The party rode horse back across the State to Louisiana, Pike County, near the spot selected for the deadly encounter, known then as Chenal Ecarti, on the Mississippi River. All stopped at an old hostelry, wearied with the trip, and sought rejuvenation in that elixir that either makes friends or enemies of those who touch glasses. They stood elbow to elbow and man to man as the glasses clicked together; and as their hearts warmed their hands clasped in friendship, and the duel was indefinitely postponed.

Verily, "All's well that ends well."

CHAPTER VII

THE MOTHER LODGE OF THE MISSISSIPPI VALLEY

"MOTHER of Lodges" was Western Star Lodge No. 107, chartered by the Grand Lodge of Pennsylvania in 1805. Western Star Lodge was truly named, for the Masonic light which it diffused was the only beacon which existed for the Masonic traveler in the whole Mississippi Valley, at that time a vast wilderness with but few settlements.

The location of this isolated lodge was Kaskaskia, Indiana Territory, then a trading post at the extreme edge of civilization, and adjoining the newly acquired Louisiana Purchase. Kaskaskia was located on the Mississippi River almost opposite the present city of St. Genevieve, Missouri, destined to be the home of the second lodge in the Valley. Kaskaskia early came into prominence through the expedition of Gen. George Rogers Clark of Revolutionary War fame, and later as the first capital of the State of Illinois.

The lodge was composed of the leading men of the community, Missourians being in the majority according to the returns for the first year. Conspicuous among the applicants for a warrant was Col. Rufus Easton, pioneer lawyer, Territorial judge and Attorney for the Territory, later appointed by President Monroe as Postmaster at St. Louis, the first Postmaster to be appointed west of the Mississippi River. Easton was born in Connecticut, and moved later to Rome, N. Y., where he joined Roman Lodge No. 82.

The question of the formation of a lodge was foremost in the minds of the small handful of rugged citizens struggling for a foothold in the tiny settlement in the Mississippi River bottoms. Meetings were held and a request for a dispensation or warrant was drawn up and signed by seven Master Masons. Three of the signers were then members of Pennsylvania lodges, one, James Edgar, having been at one time Master of his lodge at Philadelphia. As he possessed an intimate acquaintance with several members of the Grand Lodge of Pennsylvania, it was natural that the request be made of this Grand Lodge.

The application, transmitted to Grand Lodge by messenger, is so out of the ordinary and so unusual as to attract attention.

To the R. W. Grand Lodge of Pennsylvania—
Greeting:

The subscribers, and many others of our brethren in the counties of St. Clair and Randolph, beg to approach your worshipful body and state to you that they are far removed from those social enjoyments which they once as Masons have experienced; that from the growth of population many worthy and respectable brethren have settled, and many more will soon come to this country; and that your suppliants, from a sense of duty incumbent on them as Masons and as men, to promote their mutual happiness, the happiness of their neighbors, and as far as in their power lies, humanize society; and furthermore, to impress on their memory what has long been written on their hearts. Wherefore, your suppliants thus presume to approach your worshipful body and request that, if in your councils you think it expedient, your worshipful body will grant to your suppliants a warrant, or if that can't be obtained, a dispensation, authorizing them to hold a regular lodge in the town of Kaskaskia, appointing such of your suppliants to preside therein as may seem proper to your worshipful body, sending with the said warrant your constitution, all other necessary instructions and the amount of expenses attending the same, which will be duly remitted by your suppliants, etc., etc.

(Signed)   ROBERT MCMAHAN,
                 Stanton, No. 13.
             WM. ARUNDEL,
                 St. Andrews' Lodge, No. 2, *Quebec.*
             JAMES EDGAR,
                 Lodge No. 9, *Philadelphia.*
             MICHAEL JONES,
                 No. 45, *Pittsburg.*

JAMES GILBREATH,
   No. 79, Chambersburg.
RUFUS EASTON,
   Roman Lodge, No. 82, New York.
ROBT. ROBINSON,
   Stanton, No. 13,
Indiana Territory, Kaskaskia, March 9th, 1805.

The application met with favorable reception at the hands of the Grand Master of Pennsylvania, who forthwith ordered the Grand Secretary to issue the following Dispensation:

We, Israel Israel, Esquire, R. W. Grand Master of Masons in and for the Commonwealth of Pennsylvania, and Masonic jurisdiction thereunto belonging:

To all Free and Accepted Masons, wherever dispersed—Greeting:

Reposing the greatest confidence in the zeal, and constancy in the Craft of our worthy and beloved Brother James Edgar, a Past Master, Ancient York Mason, residing at Kaskaskia, in the Indiana Territory, in the United States, and by virtue of the powers and authorities vested in us, we do hereby authorize and empower and request him to call to his assistance a sufficient number of known and approved Master Masons to open a Lodge at the town of Kaskaskia aforesaid, and then and there initiate, pass, and raise Freemasons according to the most ancient and honorable custom of the Craft in all ages and nations throughout the Known World, and not contrarywise, and to make report to us hereon endorsed of their proceedings. This

Dispensation to remain in force six months from the date hereof, and no longer.

{ Seal of the Grand Lodge of Pennsylvania. } Given under our hand and the seal of the Grand Lodge at the City of Philadelphia, this 24th day of September, in the year of our Lord 1805, and in the year of Masonry 5805.

(Signed) Israel Israel, *Grand Master.*
Attest: (Signed) Geo. A. Baker, *Grand Secretary.*

Due to conditions of travel, the dispensation did not reach Kaskaskia until December, almost three months following its issue. The first Saturday (December 14, 1806) after it had been received by James Edgar the members of the proposed lodge gathered to discuss proposed by-laws, officers, and a name for the lodge.

James Edgar presided as Master, Rufus Easton as Senior Warden, Michael Jones as Junior Warden, and the remaining brethren filled the other stations, whereupon a lodge of Entered Apprentices was opened, business at that time being transacted in the first degree. The matter of naming the lodge was left to Rufus Easton and Michael Jones, and their decision (Western Star) was approved; subscriptions were taken to pay for the expenses, it being understood that all should be reimbursed for monies advanced from funds as received.

Michael Jones and Robert Robinson were appointed to prepare by-laws and report their progress to the lodge.

The first petitions to be received were those of three well-known Missourians: Andrew Henry, Walter Fenwick, and George Bullitt. Later came Chas. Querey, John Hays, John Hay, Francois Valle, Louis Lasouse Moreau, Stephen Foster, George Foster, Jas. Moore, General Henry Dodge, Thomas Oliver, Benj. Young, James Dunlap and J. Finney.

Many notable characters and distinguished names appear on the records of this lodge as members, or visitors, in addition to those above enumerated. One of the earliest visitors was Hon. John Scott of Melchisedec Lodge No. 17, New Madrid, La. Scott was later Delegate to Congress (1817) and after the admission of Missouri as a State he became the first Representative to Congress.

On March 24, 1806, Thomas F. Riddick, fifteen years later to be made Grand Master of the Grand Lodge of Missouri, was reported as a visitor from Solomon Lodge No. 30 (Va.).

Isaac Darnielle visited the lodge March 16-17 of the year 1806.

Shadrach Bond, later to become the first Governor of Illinois, as well as the first Grand Master of the Grand Lodge of Illinois, visited the lodge October 4, 1806, signing himself a member of Registerstown Lodge, Baltimore County, Maryland. Bond later affiliated with Western Star Lodge.

Captain Otho Shrader of St. Genevieve, Mo., was a frequent visitor; he was a member of Lodge No. 84, Somerset County, Pa. Shrader was an Austrian and fought under the Archduke Charles; he later became Master of Louisiana Lodge No. 109 across the river.

Aaron Burr, seeking to establish a new Republic west of the Mississippi, visited the lodge April 4, 1812, and found five brethren in attendance; he registered as a member of Union Lodge No. 40, Connecticut.

The dispensation, granted for a period of six months, being about to expire, the proceedings had under it were prepared and forwarded to Philadelphia for the approval of the Grand Lodge; the papers were accompanied by the following petition:

Kaskaskia, April 13, 1806.
To the R. W. Grand Master and Brethren of the R. W. Grand Lodge of Pa.:

Brethren:—We the subscribers, members of a Lodge holden at Kaskaskia under a dispensation granted by order of your worshipful body, in pursuance of our former petition, beg to solicit a fulfillment of your promise contained in your letter accompanied by your said dispensation, directed to Brother James Edgar, of granting a warrant and dispensation to constitute a Lodge at Kaskaskia, to be styled the Western Star Lodge. Brothers James Edgar, Michael Jones, and James Gilbreath, M.M., and formerly members of Lodges constituted under the authority of the Grand Lodge of Pennsylvania (as will more fully appear by a reference to the communications made to your worshipful body, by the several Lodges of which they have been members) have been elected officers of this Lodge, for the time being, to whom the warrant may issue. Assurances having been given by Brother James Edgar, that Brother Robert Robinson has regularly passed the chair, we do therefore desire that the dispensation for constituting the Lodge may be directed to him. Your dispensation with our proceedings endorsed thereon, as also the amount of your fees, you will find herewith enclosed.

     We are R. W. Sir and Brethren,
      yours fraternally,
(*Signed*) JAS. EDGAR, W. M.
    MICHAEL JONES, S. W.
    JAS. GILBREATH, J. W.
    ROBT. ROBINSON, *Treasurer*.
    WM. ARUNDEL, *Secretary*.

The petition was accompanied by the following certificate and recommendation:

We the subscribers, formerly members of Lodges constituted under the authority of the Grand Lodge of Pennsylvania, and present members of Western Star Lodge at Kaskaskia, do recommend the prayer of the foregoing petition to the consideration of the W. M. and members of the Grand Lodge of Pennsylvania.

       (*Signed*)   Jas. Edgar,
                          Michael Jones,
                          Jas. Gilbreath.

Recommended by
    Andrew Wilson, P. M. No. 9,
    John Boyd, P. M. No. 2,
    Jas. Wilkins, P. M. No. 9.

We do certify that Brother Robert Robinson has proved himself to us, a P. M. of a warranted Lodge of Ancient Y. M.

       (*Signed*)   Jas. Edgar,
                          Jas. Gilbreath.

The petition of April 13, 1806, reached the Grand Lodge in time for its Communication, June 3, 1806, and action is recorded in the minutes of that date:

The return to a Dispensation granted by the late R. W. Grand Master on the 24th day of September last, directed to Brother James Edgar, authorizing him to open and hold a Lodge at Kaskaskia, in the Indiana Territory, in the United States, for the term of six months from the date of said Dispensation, was read; also a letter from Brother Edgar, dated 14th April last, respecting their proceedings under said Dispensation, and also a petition from Brother Edgar and several other brethren who had been members of said Lodge held under the aforesaid Dispensation, praying for a warrant for holding a Lodge at Kaskaskia aforesaid, to be called the Western Star Lodge, and that Brother

James Edgar might be named Master, Brother Michael Jones, Senior Warden, and Brother James Gilbreath, Junior Warden of the same.

Which petition being duly recommended according to the regulations of this Grand Lodge, on motion made and seconded.

Resolved, That the prayer of the petitioners be granted, and that the Grand Secretary make out warrant accordingly, and the same be numbered 107.

In accordance with the action of the Grand Lodge the Grand Secretary prepared and forwarded the Warrant (or Charter) reading:

We, James Milnor, Esq., R. W. Grand Master of Masons in and for the Commonwealth of Pennsylvania, and the Masonic jurisdiction thereunto belonging:

To Bro. Robt. Robinson, a Past Master Mason,—
Greeting:

Reposing the greatest confidence in your zeal, fervor, and constancy in the Craft, We do, by virtue of the Powers and Authorities in Us vested, hereby authorize and empower you to call to your assistance a sufficient number of known and approved Past Master Masons to open and constitute a new Lodge at Kaskaskia, in the Indiana Territory, in the U. S., and there to proceed to the Installation of our worthy Bro. James Edgar, Master elect, and other officers of a new Lodge there to be established and constituted, to be called the "Western Star Lodge" number one hundred and seven according to the most ancient honorable custom of the Royal Craft in all ages and amongst all nations throughout the Known World, and not contrarywise, and make report to us hereon endorsed of your proceedings. This dispensation to remain in force three months from the date thereof.

{ Seal of the GRAND LODGE } Given under our hand and the seal of the R. W. Grand Lodge of Pennsylvania, at the City of Philadelphia, this 18th day of June, in the year of our Lord, 1806, and of Masonry 5806.

(*Signed*) JAS. MILNOR, *Grand Master.*
Attest: GEO. A. BAKER, *Grand Secretary.*

Brother Robert Robinson, three months later (Saturday, September 13, 1806):

Called to his assistance Brother James Gilbreath, as Senior Warden; and William Arundel, Junior Warden; when a Past Masters' Lodge was opened, and Brother James Edgar was installed as Master of said (Western Star No. 107) Lodge. The Past Masters' Lodge was closed and by virtue of a warrant from the Right Worshipful, the Grand Lodge of Pennsylvania, dated the second day of June, 1806, creating the lodge at Kaskaskia, in the Indiana Territory, called the Western Star Lodge No. 107, a Master Masons' Lodge was opened in due form.

By a certificate forwarded October 20, 1806, Bro. Robinson notified the Grand Lodge of his action in constituting the lodge.

The Committee on By-laws, consisting of Brothers Bullitt, Jones, Robinson, Fisher, Henry and Arundel, which was appointed on

October 4, 1806, was almost two years in reporting, evidence that there has been little change in the general character of committees during the past 100 years! Since these are the first by-laws established by a lodge in the Mississippi Valley, and because they afford an insight into many of the customs of lodges of that day, the substance of each section is quoted:

BYE-LAWS FOR THE GOVERNMENT OF THE WESTERN STAR LODGE No. 107, ADOPTED ST. JOHN'S DAY, 24TH JUNE, A.L., 5808, AT KASKASKIA:

Whereas, it is essential to the Beauty, Harmony and Strength of our Ancient Society that the Laws and Regulations for the government of every Individual Lodge be established agreeably to the first principles and also that those first Principles be declared in the Regulations, as well to keep them in perpetual remembrance by the members of the Lodge as to give information to all who may be desirous to join themselves in the bond of Masonry:

Be it therefore known, That to become a Brother of our Ancient Craft, a belief in the Eternal God as the Great Architect of the Universe is the first Great Essential.

A Mason is to observe the moral law, and in no case to act against the great inward light of his own conscience.

He must avoid the errors of bigotry and superstition, making use of his own reason according to that liberty wherewith he is made free.

He must allow liberty of conscience to all men; having Charity and Brotherly Love for all.

He must be a good citizen of the State in which he lives, as his obligations thereto will be greatly enforced by his duty as a Mason. He is to be a lover of quiet, and obedient to the civil powers, so far as they infringe not his bounds of reason.

Treason he must not be concerned in, nor privy to plots against the State, but consider the welfare of his country the peculiar care of a Mason. He must be industrious, and not eat any man's bread for naught.

He must endeavor to abstain from all malice and slander, and cheerfully obey those set over him, on account of their superior qualifications, however they may be inwardly ranked, for as a Free and Accepted Mason, pre-eminence of virtue and knowledge he is to consider as the only standard of true nobility.

He must know himself capable of keeping secrets, as it is conferred upon him by the strongest obligations.

He must be free born, of the age of twenty-one years, of good report, of sufficient natural endowments, with the sense of a man, with an estate, office, trade, or occupation, or some known way of acquiring an honest "livelyhood." He must be upright in body, not deformed or dismembered, but of hale and entire limbs, as a man ought to be.

And for the more immediate well ordering and conducting of this lodge, it is hereby ordained by the Master, Wardens, and brethren thereof, at this their communication.

Section 1. Provides that the meetings shall be held on the first Saturday of each month, from seven to ten o'clock between March 25th and September 25th, and from six to nine between September 25th and March 25th.

Section 2. Provides for election of officers—Worshipful Master, Senior and Junior Wardens, and Treasurer.

Section 3. Provides that, with the consent of the Lodge, the W. M. may appoint two Deacons, the Secretary, and a Steward, and provides that if either of the brethren so appointed shall refuse to serve, he shall pay one dollar, unless he had served in a similar office before, in which case the W. M. make a new appointment.

Section 4. Provides for the duties of the Treasurer—all the receipts of the lodge being paid directly to him.

Section 5. In a like manner defines the duties of the Secretary.

Section 6. Provides for proper order and decorum when the Master takes the chair, and while the Lodge is in session.

Section 7. Provides for the manner of putting and deciding question before the Lodge.

Section 8. Provides that a brother may call for the previous question, and the question put, if the motion is seconded and thirded.

Section 10. No brother shall rise to speak or interrupt another addressing the Master, unless to call to order; or if any shall mock, deride, or endeavor to ridicule any brother whilst speaking, or while the Lodge is sitting, he shall, on conviction by a majority of the members present forfeit and pay for the first offense five dollars, and ask pardon of the Lodge and of the offended brother; for the second offense he shall forfeit and pay ten dollars, and ask pardon of the Lodge and the offended brother; for the third offense he shall foreit and pay fifteen dollars, and ask pardon of the Lodge and the offended brother, and for the fourth offense shall be expelled, and not be re-admitted without the unanimous consent of the Lodge, to be given either by ballot or otherwise, as the Lodge shall determine, and shall pay twenty dollars to the Charity fund.

Section 11. Provides that the Master shall be the judge of all questions of order.

Section 12. Provides that a brother cursing or swearing, or holding an angry dispute, shall be subject to the same penalties as prescribed in section ten.

Section 13. That no brother shall improperly harass by suit or suits at law, any other brother of this or any other Lodge, but shall at all times, whenever a dispute exists, give a fair and reasonable opportunity of settling the same in an amicable manner.

Section 14. Provides that any brother revealing any of the transactions of the Lodge shall be fined fifteen dollars, or be expelled, and if expelled, should "not be re-admitted at all."

Section 15. Provides for the appointment of a Tyler, and defines his duties. In the Tyler's absence the duty devolved upon the "youngest brother present to tyle the Lodge, who shall do the duty of Tyler without reward, under the penalty of five dollars, unless sufficient reason be assigned."

Section 16. Appropriates all fines and forfeitures to the Charity fund.

Section 17. Provides that each and every member pay one dollar and eighty-four cents at each festival of St. John the Evangelist, one dollar for the Charity fund, and eighty-four cents for the Grand Lodge. The penalty for non-payment of dues was expulsion; provided, two-thirds of the members present concurred in such motion. Provides for the withdrawal of members, and serving of notices on members delinquent.

Section 18. Provides that every brother and visitor shall pay to the Treasurer before retiring from the lodge room, twenty-five cents for refreshments; and every absent brother was liable to a like charge.

MOTHER LODGE OF MISSISSIPPI VALLEY

Section 19. In regard to visiting brethren.

Section 20. Provides for the affiliation of members, and the fees therefor. If a Master Mason wished to affiliate, the fee was four dollars; if an F. C. eight dollars; if an E. A. ten dollars, which fee in the latter case probably entitled the brethren to advancement; one half of such fees to the Charity fund, and the other to the Contingent fund.

Section 21. Provides for the reception, referring, report upon, and balloting upon petitions for initiation, and the fees. The brother initiated paid to the Charity fund eight dollars, to the Contingent fund eight dollars, to the Secretary one dollar, one dollar to the Tyler, and one dollar for the Grand Lodge dues—nineteen dollars, which sum it is supposed included the degrees of F. C. and M. M.

Section 22. No monies shall ever be taken from the Charity fund to pay any Contingent expenses of the Lodge, without the consent of two-thirds of the brethren present.

Section 23. Whenever the Charity fund exceeded one hundred dollars, it was to be loaned.

Section 24. Provided for the amendment or alteration of these By-Laws.

Section 25. Provided that every member shall sign the By-Laws.

Section 26. All motions to expel a member shall be made at a stated Lodge night, and grounded on written charges, which shall be laid before the Lodge, a certified copy of which charge shall be delivered (if within reach of the Lodge) at least one month before the question shall be taken by the Lodge thereon, and the party so charged shall at the same time be notified to make his defense in writing (if within reach of the Lodge), accompanied with such proofs as he may think necessary to his defense: Provided, however, that the testimony of any person not a member of this, or any other regular Lodge, and in presence of at least two disinterested Masons agreed upon and nominated by the parties, giving the opposite party a reasonable notice (if within the reach of the Lodge) of the time and place of taking such testimony.

Provided, also, that if a member be reported to be not within the reach of this Lodge (by the report of the Secretary in conformity to the above rule), the proceedings shall be had against him, as though he were within the jurisdiction of the Lodge.

Signed by MICHAEL JONES, W. M.; R. ROBINSON, S. W.; GEORGE FISHER, J. W.; JAMES DUNLAP, TREASURER; WILLIAM ARUNDEL, SEC.; J. FINNEY, S. D.; DAVID ROBINSON, J. D.; JAMES EDGAR, J. GILBREATH, JOHN HAYS, JAMES HALL, SR., JOHN HAY, NATHAN DAVIS, T. TUTTLE, JAMES HALL, JR., SHADRACH BOND, JR., ENOCH PAINE, HENRY CONNOR, BYRD LOCKHART, JR., J. A. BOYES, THOMAS C. BROWNE, THOS. TODD, WM. BENNETT, WHARTON RECTOR, T. G. R. RHEA, CALD. W. CAIRNES, K. BARTON, JAMES B. MOORE, CHARLES McPHERSON, PHILIP FOUKE, JESSE W. COOPER, W. FENWICK, WARREN BROWN, WM. G. GREENUP, JAMES M. DUNCAN, L. LaCHAPELLE, SAMUEL OMELVENY, THOMAS FERGUSON, JACOB FEAMAN, E. OWEN, JOHN BIVINS, JOHN H. ROBINSON, JOHN GILLISS, WM. McDONALD, SAMUEL C. CHRISTY, DAVID SCOTT, 3RD., JOHN W. NELSON, PHILIP TRAMELL, JOHN WALLS, THOMAS C. PATTERSON, JAMES S. CHEEK, CLEMENT C. CONWAY, HENRY S. DODGE, HIPOLITE MENARD, JEPTHA SWEET, DANIEL S. SWEARINGEN, ROBERT LATTY, PHILIP ROCHEBLAVE, THOMAS REYNOLDS, SAMUEL WALKER, SAMUEL SMITH, DAVID ANDERSON, EDMUND ROBERTS, WM. BOON, JOSIAH T.

Betts, William McBride, Jesse Griggs, Seth Converse, Alexander Phillips, Samuel Whiteside, James Clark, Martin Jones, William Alexander, Beal Greenup, John N. Robinson, John Atkins, Ferdinand Onjer, Andrew Buckham, Thomas Brady, John Latty, T. J. V. Owen, D. C. Taggart, Amos Anderson.

Although far from civilization, life in the great west was not without its thrills, as the records of March 6, 1812, will testify:

Four brethren present; the lodge opened on the first degree. The minutes of the last stated night called for, it was found that no lodge was held—that the earthquakes, so frequent and alarming at the time, rendered an essemblage of the members almost impossible, and indeed unsafe. The stone house in which the lodge was kept was considerably shattered by the frequent concussions, and was on that evening abandoned by its proprietor, Brother Greenup, who from the hurry of the moment, in moving his family, forgot to make any arrangements. The books and furniture then became inaccessible to those who had met and consequently the delinquency on the part of the lodge in not meeting was unavoidable.

In which the Grand Lodge of Pennsylvania no doubt concurred!

The granting of Diplomas or Certificates, while not common, was not altogether unusual; typical of those issued by Western Star Lodge is that issued to William Arundel, *Junior War-*

den, and for many years Secretary of the Lodge. It reads:

SUMMA LAUS DEO.

In the East arose a light, and the light shineth in darkness, and the darkness comprehendeth it not.

We, the Master and Wardens of Western Star Lodge No. 107, Ancient York Masons, held in the town of Kaskaskia, in the Illinois Territory, under a regular charter from the Worshipful Grand Lodge of Pennsylvania, do hereby certify that Brother William Arundel, who hath signed his name in the margin, and unto whom we grant these letters, is a regular and duly Registered Master Mason, and has performed all his works amongst us to the entire satisfaction of his brethren. We therefore pray all the Worshipful Lodges and all Free and Accepted Masons to receive him into Fellowship wherever Providence may allot his abode on Earth.

In testimony whereof we have hereto set our hands, countersigned by our said Brother and Secretary (no seal for our lodge being yet provided), at Kaskaskia, this twenty-second day of June, Anno Lucis 5812.

P. FOUKE, *Master.*
WM. C. GREENUP, *S. Warden.*
JAMES EDGAR, *J. Warden.*

MICH'L JONES, *Sec'y. P. T.*

Dimit, in addition to certifying to the Masonic standing, recounted the numerous virtues of its possessor, as witness the following granted March 2, 1816, to Brother Philip Rocheblave:

Western Star Lodge No. 107.

To all Free and Accepted Masons; Union, Health, and Happiness:

We, the Masters and Wardens of Western Star Lodge No. 107, held at Kaskaskia, in the County of Randolph, under the Grand Warrant of Pennsylvania assembled in Due form adorned with all our honors, do hereby declare and attest to all men enlightened on the face of the earth, that our beloved Brother Philip Rocheblave, who hath signed his name in the margin, hath been received as an entered apprentice, passed as a fellow craft; and after having sustained with firmness, strength, and courage, the most painful works and wonderful trials, we have given to him as a recompense, due to his zeal, diligence, and capacity, the sublime degree of Master, and have admitted and initiated him as such into our mysteries and secret works in which he has helped us with his talents, skill and knowledge. In testimony whereof, we have granted to him this present certificate, signed by our Master and Wardens, and attested by our Secretary, with the private seal of the said lodge, the twenty-fifth day of April, in the year of Masonry 5816, and of Salvation 1816.

    S. BOND, W. M.
    P. FOUKE, S. W.
    SAMUEL WALKER, J. W.
Attest: D. S. SWEARINGEN, *Secretary*.

The celebration of the Anniversaries of St. John the Baptist and St. John the Evangelist were carried out punctiliously, offering occasion for public appearance and procession; these ceremonies usually consisted of the assembling of all members of the lodge at their lodge-room, a march to some public assembly-room, a sermon by a minister or often some competent brother, and a sumptuous dinner served at the home of one of the active members.

The only other occasion for public appearance was at funerals of deceased members; a glimpse is had of some of the customs of lodges by reference to the minutes:

> Resolved, that the members of this lodge will, as a token of their grief for the death of their deceased brother, N. G. R. Rhea, wear a piece of black ribbon through the second and third button-holes of their coats for three months.

November 1, 1817, James Edgar, who more than any other man was responsible for the organizing of Western Star Lodge, died. The lodge held a regular meeting on this evening to make arrangement for the funeral obsequies. The records state, on this occasion:

> The lodge being informed that Brother James Edgar, a member of this lodge, departed this life on the morning of this day, passed the following resolve:
> "Resolved, That the members of this lodge will meet at the lodge-room on the morrow at one o'clock, and proceed therefrom to the house of their deceased brother, James Edgar, long a member, and one of the founders of the lodge, and attend the funeral, and pay him Masonic honors; and that the members of Louisiana Lodge No. 109,

St. Genevieve, be invited to attend at Kaskaskia at three o'clock on to-morrow evening, and that a special messenger be engaged by the Treasurer to carry the notice and information to the Louisiana Lodge in such way as the Worshipful Master may direct."

On the following day (Sunday), fifteen members of the fraternity assembled to do the last honors to one who had labored zealously for the Craft; the lodge was opened on the third degree, proceeded to the home of the deceased and thence to the place of interment "where the body was buried with Masonic honors."

The last minutes of Lodge No. 107 are those of December 9, 1820, but certain records, yet in existence, lead us to believe that meetings were held as late as the year 1829. The antimasonic excitement which developed at this period was no doubt responsible for its demise. Western Star, which in 1806, gave forth such promise, was now dropping below the Masonic horizon, never to rise again; for almost a quarter of a century it had furnished the light by which Master Masons of the Mississippi Valley had guided their steps. Its light was the inspiration for thousands of lodges during the next century; it was the forerunner—the mother—of such lodges as Louisiana No. 109,

St. Louis No. 111, and a host of other lodges chartered during this and later periods.

Like the Sprig of Acacia, emblem of immortality, let the name of Western Star Lodge remind us that the work of these pioneer Freemasons will live always. All hail then, to Western Star Lodge, the beacon light which shone at the edge of the wilderness, leading men from darkness to light, bringing those who were blind by ways that they knew not, and making crooked paths straight as best they knew.

Such was the work of Western Star. Today, but a few scattered records are all that remain to mark the existence of this lodge, even the site of which is to-day covered by the Great Father of Waters, as if in testimony of the mortality of worldly things.

CHAPTER VIII

THE STORY OF LOUISIANA LODGE NO. 109

SAINT GENEVIEVE, founded about the year 1735, is the oldest settlement in Missouri Territory; when Pierre Laclede, August and Peter Chouteau received a permit in 1763 to trade with the Indians along the Upper Mississippi, and set out with their families and possessions, Saint Genevieve was their destination. On their arrival they found it less satisfactory than territory north of St. Genevieve, so they finally settled at the present site of St. Louis, which had the additional advantage of being nearer the mouth of the Missouri River.

At the time of the transfer of the Territory to the United States, in 1804, Saint Genevieve was the most important village on the west bank of the Mississippi, its only rival being Kaskaskia, on the opposite side, in Indiana Territory. Kaskaskia was composed largely of English settlers, while Saint Genevieve was made up of French and Spanish. With the new government came English traders and pioneers, many of the inhabitants of Kaskaskia taking land claims on the Missouri side, while the English language and customs began slowly to replace those of the French and Spanish.

The first lodge in the Mississippi Valley was at Kaskaskia. Western Star Lodge was the Mother Lodge of the whole Valley, drawing members not only from Kaskaskia, but from Cahokia, St. Louis and Saint Genevieve. The first annual returns of this lodge show fully half of its members resident in the new Territory.

The rapid growth of the new settlement and the difficulties of crossing the Mississippi, especially at night and often during the high water and ice floes, caused the resident Masons to long for a lodge nearer their homes. Besides the members of Western Star Lodge, a number of settlers in Louisiana Territory still retained membership in lodges on the Atlantic Coast, men who had received their degrees previous to coming West. Those engaged in business often had occasion to journey to Philadelphia, where they came in touch with members of the Grand Lodge of Pennsylvania; thus many of the early pioneers became members of Pennsylvania lodges.

Aaron Elliott, the pioneer American physician, came to St. Genevieve about the year 1798, as land records show that he purchased a tract of land that year from Maxwell the Curé; he was not a member of Western Star Lodge, although he signed the petition for dispensation, and was named as Worshipful Master of the first lodge at St. Genevieve. His family was closely allied with the old established families, one daughter marrying Wm. C. Carr, and another (Marie Louise Elliott) marrying Leon Delassus, son of Camille Delassus. Otho Shrader, another of the charter members of the lodge, was not a member of Western Star Lodge, but very active in the formation of the new lodge. Shrader settled in St. Genevieve about 1806; he was a German-Austrian from Sunbury, Pa., and President Thomas Jefferson, who was familiar with his ability, appointed him as a Territorial judge. His death occurred in 1811, in St. Louis, while in attendance upon a council of governors and judges. History states that he had been a soldier in Austria, under the Archduke Charles, before coming to America. His training and ability made him a good organizer and executive, and his hand and brain are seen in many of the actions of the lodge and in the plans for its formation.

Judge Otho Shrader gathered together

Masons resident in Saint Genevieve, and with the full consent of the Mother Lodge, applied to the Grand Lodge of Pennsylvania for a dispensation to meet as a lodge and confer the three degrees of Ancient Craft Masonry upon residents of the new Territory, when they should regularly petition and be found worthy. To Worshipful Brother Shrader is due the credit for planting the first Masonic Lodge in the Mississippi Valley, west of the great "Father of Waters."

During the fifteen years of the existence of this lodge, it numbered among its members seventy-five of the leading citizens of the Territory, many of whom dimitted to form lodges at St. Louis, Herculaneum, Potosi and Jackson. Louisiana Lodge No. 109 is therefore the Mother Lodge of all Missouri Lodges as well as many lodges chartered in other States.

A meeting having been held to consider the matter of the formation of a new lodge, the following application for a dispensation was drawn up and signed by nine Master Masons and two Entered Apprentices:

To the Right Worshipful Grand Master, Grand Officers and Members of the Right Worshipful Grand Lodge of Pennsylvania.

The subscribers, regular members of the Society of Ancient York Masons and residing in the Territory of Louisiana,

Respectfully represent

That they are desirous of forming themselves into a lodge to be held in the Town of St. Genevieve in the said Territory of Louisiana under the sanction of the Right Worshipful Grand Lodge of Pennsylvania; for which purpose they beg to nominate Brother Doctor Aaron Elliott, a regular Past Master, as Master, Brother Andrew Henry, a regular Master Mason, as Senior Warden, and Brother George Bullitt, a regular Master Mason, as Junior Warden, of such lodge, and pray the said Right Worshipful Grand Lodge to grant them a Warrant to open and hold a lodge in the said Town of St. Genevieve, under the name of "The Louisiana Lodge."

The subscribers also inform the Right Worshipful Grand Lodge that this memorial is accompanied with the money requisite for obtaining the said Warrant, and further beg leave to recommend that their much respected Brother James Edgar, now Worshipful Master of the Western Star Lodge No. 107, held at Kaskaskia, in the Territory of Indiana, may be authorized and deputed to open such lodge and install the before named Brethren into their respective offices according to the ancient rules of Free Masonry.

The subscribers entertain the flattering hope that this institution will prosper and promote the benefits of Free Masonry under the auspices of the Right Worshipful

Grand Lodge of Pennsylvania for which they feel happy of this opportunity to acknowledge their high esteem and regard.

St. Genevieve, December 27th, 1806.

Aaron Elliott, P. M.
Andrew Henry, M.
Geo. Bullitt, M.
Robert Terry, M.
John Hepburn (?) M.
Thomas F. Riddick, M.
Otho Shrader, P. M.
H. Dodge, E. A.
Tho. Oliver, E. A.
Louis Lassous, M.
Francois Valle, M.

The application was accompanied by a waiver of jurisdiction from Western Star Lodge No. 107, which at that time appeared to have jurisdiction over this Territory. Notwithstanding No. 107, by this action, would lose almost half its members, it willingly gave its consent; the waiver was signed by the officers of No. 107, and transmitted with the other papers to the Grand Secretary of the Grand Lodge of Pennsylvania.

The waiver read:

At a meeting of the Western Star Lodge held at Kaskaskia in the Territory of Indiana, on St. John's Day, the 27th December A. L. 5806, James Edgar, *Worshipful Master*, in the chair.

THE STORY OF LOUISIANA LODGE NO. 109

A petition having been presented to this lodge signed by a number of ancient York Masons (to us known as such) residing at St. Genevieve and its vicinity in the Territory of Louisiana together with some members of this lodge, praying this lodge to recommend to the Right Worshipful Grand Lodge of Pennsylvania Brother Doctor Aaron Elliott as Worshipful Master, Brother Andrew Henry, as Senior Warden, and Brother George Bullitt as Junior Warden, of a lodge to be constituted in the Town of St. Genevieve in the Territory aforesaid, to be called the "Louisiana Lodge"—This lodge having had said petition under consideration Do hereby recommend the said Aaron Elliott, Andrew Henry and George Bullitt, all Master Masons, as proper characters to fill the Offices aforesaid, agreeable to the prayer of the petition hereto annexed.

In testimony whereof we, the W. Master and Wardens of the said Western Star Lodge No. 107, held under the jurisdiction of the R. W. Grand Lodge of Pennsylvania at Kaskaskia aforesaid, have hereunto set our hands and seals the day and year above written.

      JAMES EDGAR, W. M. Seal
      MICH'L JONES, S. W. Seal
      JAS. GILBREATH, J. W. Seal

N.B. Nine of the foregoing petitioners are known to us as Master Masons.

No seal being procured the Private Seal is substituted.
Attest:
 WILLIAM ARUNDEL,
   Secretary.

The petition and accompanying waiver were sent by messenger to Philadelphia; although both were dated "December 27th, 1806," they did not reach their destination until July 1807, at a time when the Grand Lodge was "in vacation."

The Grand Master was willing to assist his brethren of the Far West by calling a Special Communication of the Grand Lodge, so that the messenger might carry back with him the necessary lawful authority to carry on the work. We read in the official minutes of the Grand Lodge of Pennsylvania that a "Grand Extra Communication" was held on Friday, July 17, 1807, and that the following proceedings were noted by George A. Baker, Grand Secretary:

> The R. W. Grand Master informed the Brethren that they had been convened for the purpose of taking into consideration a Petition praying for a Warrant for holding a lodge.
> Said Petition was thereupon read.
> It was from several Brethren residing in the Territory of Louisiana praying for a Warrant for holding a lodge in the Town of St. Genevieve in the said Territory to be called "The Louisiana Lodge" and that Brother Doctor Aaron Elliott might be named Master; Brother Andrew Henry, Senior Warden, and Brother George Bullitt, Junior Warden of the same; and that Brother James Edgar, W. M. of the Western Star Lodge No. 107, held at Kaskaskia might be authorized to constitute the said lodge.

THE STORY OF LOUISIANA LODGE NO. 109

Which Petition being in due form and being recommended by said Lodge No. 107, agreeably to the Regulations of this Grand Lodge, it was on Motion made and seconded, Resolved, That the prayer of the Petitioners be granted, and that Brother Grand Secretary make out a Warrant accordingly, and that the said lodge be Number 109.

Grand Lodge adjourned in Harmony at 9 o'clock P.M.

This action of the Grand Lodge of Pennsylvania was the first record of the granting of a warrant or dispensation to a lodge west of the Mississippi River, and this but three years following the acquisition of Louisiana Territory by the United States.

It is not to be supposed that a Communication of a Grand Lodge can be held without some expense and a *"Grand Extra* Communication" was no exception; the expense of such, agreeably to custom, is chargeable to the lodge in whose interest said Extra Communication is held.

The official statement of the Grand Lodge of Pennsylvania of the amount due for "Warrant" and other expenses makes interesting reading:

Lodge No. 109.
To the Grand Lodge of Pennsylvania, Dr.

1807
July 29th—To cost of Warrant for holding said
    lodge including Secretary's Fee $60—$4 ... $64.—
    To dispensation to Constitute............   7.—
    To Grand Tyler's account for carrying
    notices, Tyling inside and outside and Can-
    dles—it having been a Special Meeting
    called for the purpose of receiving the Peti-
    tion for said Warrant................   5.—

                                                                    $76.—

                Errors & Omissions Excepted
                    GEORGE A. BAKER,
                            Grand Secretary.

Brother Armstrong, the Grand Treasurer, received payment in full of the above account as is shown by his receipt:

September 17, 1807. Received of James Milnor, Esq., Seventy Six Dollars in full payment of the above Account and for which I have given Duplicate Receipts.
                    T. L. ARMSTRONG,
$76.—   *Treasurer of the Grand Lodge.*

The Grand Tyler presented his bill in the following form:

THE STORY OF LOUISIANA LODGE NO. 109   127

Philadelphia, July 17th, 1807.

Special G. Lodge
    To Wm. Schnider
        Tyling in and out Side................ $4.—
        Candles .... 1.—
                                                $5.—

The warrant was made out in regular form by the Grand Secretary and sent to Worshipful Brother Edgar, at Kaskaskia, with authority to constitute. The warrant reads:

JAMES MILNOR
Grand Master
FRED WOLBERT
Deputy Grand Master

ROBERT LEWIS   ROBERT POALK
Senior Grand Warden   *Junior Grand Warden*

TO ALL TO WHOM IT MAY CONCERN

THE GRAND LODGE OF PENNSYLVANIA AND MASONIC JURISDICTION Thereunto belonging, in Ample Form assembled at Philadelphia, in the Commonwealth of Pennsylvania.
WISDOM!!! STRENGTH!!! FRATERNITY!!!
KNOW YE, That We the said Grand Lodge of the most Ancient and Honorable Fraternity of Free and Accepted Masons (according to the Old Constitutions, revived by his Royal Highness Prince Edwin, at York, in the Kingdom of England, in the Year of the Christian Aera Nine Hundred Twenty and Six, and in the Year of Masonry

Four Thousand Nine Hundred Twenty and Six) by Virtue of the Powers and Authorities vested in US, Do hereby constitute and appoint our trusty and well beloved Brethren

   Aaron Elliott, *Master*,
    Andrew Henry, *Senior Warden*, and
   George Bullitt, *Junior Warden*
    of a Lodge to be called
      The Louisiana Lodge—Number One Hundred and Nine, to be held in the Town of St. Genevieve, in the Territory of Louisiana, in the United States—or within Five Miles of the same.

And we do further authorize and empower our said trusty and well-beloved Brethren, Aaron Elliott, Andrew Henry and George Bullitt—to admit and make Freemasons according to the most Ancient and Honorable Custom of the Royal Craft in all Ages and Nations throughout the known world, and not contrarywise.

And we do further impower and appoint the said Aaron Elliott, Andrew Henry and George Bullitt—and their successors to hear and determine all and singular matters and things relating to the Craft within the Jurisdiction of the said Lodge, with the assistance of the Members of said lodge.

And lastly, we do authorize and impower our said trusty and well beloved Brethren, Aaron Elliott, Andrew Henry and George Bullitt—to install their Successors, being first duly elected and chosen, to whom they shall deliver this Warrant, and to invest them with all the Powers and Dignities to their offices respectively belonging, and such Successors shall in like manner, from time to time, install their successors, &c, &c, &c. Such installation to be upon or near St. John the Evangelist's Day, during the continuance of this lodge forever. Provided always, That the said above named Brethren, and their Successors, pay due respect to this Right Worshipful Grand Lodge and the Ordinances thereof, otherwise this Warrant to be of no Force or Effect.

                Given in open *GRAND LODGE*, under the Hands of our Right Worshipful Grand Officers and the Seal of the Grand Lodge at Philadelphia,
Seal.   this Seventeenth Day of July— A.D. One Thousand Eight Hundred and Seven—and of Masonry Five Thousand Eight Hundred and Seven.—

    THOS. ARMSTRONG,
                Grand Treasurer.

Attest:
  GEORGE A. BAKER, *Grand Secretary.*

The official instructions, for the constituting of the new lodge, were contained in the authorization issued by the Grand Master to Worshipful Brother Edgar.

WE, JAMES MILNOR, ESQUIRE, Right Worshipful Grand Master of Masons in and for the Commonwealth of Pennsylvania and Masonic Jurisdiction thereunto belonging.

To our Worthy and much Respected Brother, James Edgar, Esquire, a Past Master Mason.
GREETING:—
Reposing the greatest confidence in your Zeal, Fervor and Constancy in the Craft, We do by virtue of the Powers and authorities in US vested, hereby authorize and empower you to call to your assistance a sufficient number of known and approved Past Master Masons to open and

Constitute a New Lodge to be held in the Town of St. Genevieve in the Territory of Louisiana in the United States, and there to proceed to the installation of our Worthy Brother Aaron Elliott, Master elect, and the Other Officers of a New Lodge there to be established and Constituted, to be called "The Louisiana Lodge" Number One Hundred and Nine, according to the most ancient and Honourable Custom of the Royal Craft in all Ages and amongst all Nations throughout the Known World and not contrarywise, and make report to US hereon Endorsed of all your proceedings.

This Dispensation to remain in force for Six Months from the Date hereof and no longer.

                    Given under Our Hand and the Seal of our Right Worshipful Grand Lodge at the City of Philadelphia in the said Commonwealth of Pennsylvania, this Twenty Fourth Day of July in the year of Our LORD 1807 and of Masonry 5807.

Seal.

                                  J. MILNOR.
                    Attest:
                    GEORGE A. BAKER,
                         Grand Secretary.

That Louisiana Lodge was constituted by Worshipful Brother Edgar is evidenced by the return of the authorization to the Grand Secretary with the following notation:

To the Right Worshipful James Milnor, Esq.
    Grand Master of Masons in and for the Commonwealth of Pennsylvania & Masonic Jurisdiction thereunto belonging:

I do certify that by virtue of the within Dispensation to me directed, having called to my assistance a sufficient number of known and approved Past Master Masons, I have on the Fourteenth Day of November, One Thousand Eight Hundred and Seven, opened and constituted at the Town of St. Genevieve, in the Territory of Louisiana, in the United States, a new lodge called the "Louisiana Lodge" No. 109, and have then and there installed our Worthy Brother Aaron Elliott, Master; Andrew Henry, Senior Warden; and George Bullitt, Junior Warden, according to the most ancient and honorable customs of Masonry.

In witness whereof I have hereunto set my hand.

JAMES EDGAR.

The year in which Louisiana Lodge adopted its by-laws is not known; it is believed they were adopted shortly after the constitution of the lodge by Worshipful Brother James Edgar. A supplement to the by-laws shows that amendments were made in October 1813, and again in April 1815. It was not until 1815 that the by-laws were presented to the Grand Lodge of Pennsylvania for their approval, and the committee to whom they were referred reported their corrections January 4th, 1816.

BY-LAWS OF LOUISIANA LODGE NO. 109

ARTICLE I

Of the Meeting and Livery of the Lodge.

Section 1. This lodge shall be convened on the second

Monday in every month, and at such times as the Worshipful Master or Presiding Warden in his absence, shall judge proper.

Section 2. The half yearly communications shall be held on the feasts of St. John the Baptist and St. John the Evangelist.

Section 3. Members who live at such a distance as to render it inconvenient to attend the monthly meetings may be allowed by the lodge—to attend as quarterly or half yearly members, and shall accordingly attend the Quarterly meetings in March, June, September and December, or the half yearly meetings in June and December, and also in both cases the meetings on the days of the two Feasts, at all other times their attendance shall be at their discretion, unless specially summoned by the order of the Worshipful Master for the time then being.

Section 4. The livery of the Lodge shall be blue.

ARTICLE II

Of Called Lodge.

Section 1. A called lodge or lodge in case of emergency shall not be convened except by order of the Worshipful Master or in his absence by the presiding Warden.

Section 2. When a lodge is convened on any private account, the brother for whose benefit it was convened shall pay all the necessary expenses incurred by such extra meeting, unless the Master and Wardens shall certify that in their opinion such meeting is to be paid by and for the benefit of the lodge, in that case the expenses shall be paid by the lodge, nor shall any other business be transacted at a called meeting, but that for which the lodge was expressly called.

ARTICLE III

Of the Election of Officers.

Section 1. The Master, Wardens, Secretary and Treasurer, shall be chosen by ballot on the stated lodge night preceding St. John the Evangelist's Day and shall be duly installed on the feast of St. John the Evangelist, every member present who has paid his dues shall be entitled to vote—no person shall be elected to fill either of the aforesaid offices, unless he has a majority of all the votes given. The Deacons, Stewart & Tyler shall be appointed by the Master.

Section 2. Before any election takes place the list of members, and the delinquents shall be called over, in order to ascertain whether any member present may have forfeited his right to vote, or hold an office.

ARTICLE IV

Of the Duties of the Officers.

Section 1. It shall be the duty of the Worshipful Master at every meeting when time will permit to give the Brethren a Lecture in that Degree in which the lodge may be setting and take charge of the charter unless in case he is absent then it becomes the duty of the Presiding Warden.

The Master shall also keep due order while the lodge is open, any brother may appeal from the decision of the chair to the lodge.

Section 2. Tyler—The Secretary shall take charge of the Tools and see that they be kept bright, as also the Jewels of the lodge.

Section 3. The Treasurer shall keep a regular account

of all receipts and disbursements, and of the credits and debts of the individual members.

Section 4. At the stated meetings in June and December immediately preceding to their two feasts, the Treasurer shall lay before the lodge a list of delinquents with the account of their respective delinquencies, and the time thereof annexed to their respective names in order that the same may be read before the lodge by the Treasurer or Secretary.

Section 5. The Treasurer shall collect the monthly, quarterly and half yearly contributions, the fee for admission and introductory fee for every Degree, and shall acknowledge himself satisfied in this respect before any Degree shall be conferred.

Section 6. The Treasurer shall twice in the year, immediately after each St. John's Day render to the Master and Wardens a just and true account of all monies which shall have received into his hands and to produce vouchers for all expenditures which he has made upon orders drawn by the Master, attested by the Secretary, Provided however that no such order shall be drawn, nor any monies be paid by the Treasurer without the consent of the lodge except that which the Master and Wardens shall draw out of the Charity fund for charitable purposes the balance remaining in the Treasurer's hands shall be forthwith paid over to his successor in office and the Master and Wardens shall make report to the Lodge, the first stated meeting after the settlement had with the Treasurer.

Section 7. The Secretary on application shall deliver to any member of this lodge a Diploma drawn up in proper form, provided the said member produces the Treasurer's receipt for having discharged all lodge dues and not otherwise.

Section 8. It shall be the duty of the Tyler to see that

every Brother is cloathed according to his Degree before he enters the lodge.

ARTICLE V

Of the Business of the Lodge.

Section 1. No business shall be transacted at an Extraordinary meeting except for that which the lodge may have been convened.

Section 2. No brother who is not a Master Mason shall make or second a motion.

Section 3. At the stated meetings all business must originate and whatever belongs to the first Degree of Masonry must be transacted subject to the following resolution, namely no candidate can be balloted for or initiated on the day of the annual Election or on either of the Feast Days.

Section 4. A list of the members of the Lodge and the Bye-Laws shall be shown to every candidate and Bye-Laws shall be read to every new made brother or presented to him for his perusiall and at any other time the Worshipful Master may direct.

Section 5. No passing or raising shall take place on either of the Feast Days.

Section 6. At any time during the sitting of the Lodge which the Master may appear proper, the Secretary shall call over the list of members.

Section 7. The charter shall be shown to every new made brother, and every visitor if required.

Section 8. In all processions those Brethren who may be appointed to offices pro tempore, shall continue to fill such offices until the procession returns to the Lodge.

ARTICLE VI

Of Behavior in the Lodge.

Section 1. The Brethren shall pay due respect to the Master and Wardens on entering and retiring from the Lodge, shall observe a becoming decency in their behavior whilst in the Lodge and not depart without the permission of the Master.

Section 2. The Master shall publicly reprimand any Brother who shall commit any irregularity in decorum in open Lodge.

Section 3. As drunkenness and profaneness are atrocious and intolerable, whosoever dare violate the Congregation of the Brethren in either of those ways shall by order of the Worshipful Master be led out of the room and not permitted to return without satisfactory concession to the Lodge and for a repetition of either offence shall be punished by a suspension from all privileges of the order for three months, and for a third offence of the same kind shall be suspended from all privileges of the order.

Section 4. Every Brother in delivering his sentiments shall stand and address the Worshipful Master, shall speak with moderation and cautiously avoid flat contradiction and whosoever shall intercept a brother whilst speaking, hiss, laugh at, or in any manner ridicule what such Brother shall have advanced or hold private conference, such offender shall be deemed a disturber of the Lodge and treated accordingly.

Section 5. No Brother can expect to be heard more than twice upon the discussion of the same subject unless the Master shall give his special permission.

ARTICLE VII

Of Recommendation, Ballotting & Admission.

Section 1. To qualify a candidate for initiation, he must be of good report, free born, of mature age, whole and sound, not deformed or dismembered, but corporal deformity not rendering the candidate incapable of persuing the ordinary avocations of life, nor preventing him from procuring by his own labor a livelyhood, nor unfitting him for the exercise of his duties as a Mason shall not be an objection.

Section 2. Any person wishing to be initiated into the mysteries of Masonry must make known his request by petition to the Masters, Wardens and members of the Lodge, such petition shall be presented at some stated meeting of the Lodge and not at any adjournment or extra meeting of the Lodge, accompanied by a recommendation signed by at least two, said Law or alteration in writing to the Master after being perused by the Master it shall be read by the Secretary and if then seconded by a Master Mason it shall be over one month and shall then be determined after a full discussion when concurrence of a majority of two-thirds of the members present shall be necessary to constitute it a part of those Laws.

Section 3. Every member shall be provided with a printed copy of the Bye-Laws at the expense of the Lodge.

These Bye-Laws shall be entered by the Secretary in a Book to be procured for that purpose and every member on his admission into this Lodge shall subscribe these Laws, thereby acknowledging himself bound in every respect strictly to comply with them.

Master Masons member of the Lodge. (This petition shall (except when the candidate is very generally known in which case the committee to be herein after appointed by the Master to inquire into his character may report immediately) lie over for consideration one month at least that the members may have time to inform themselves fully of the principles, character and connections of the candidate). Whereupon the Master shall appoint a committee of three Master Masons to inquire into the character and qualifications of the candidate any two of whom shall report the result of this inquiry at the next stated meeting after their appointment in writing.

Should the report of the committee stated be favorable to the candidate he shall then be balloted for and if a single brother is found to vote against his admission he shall be rejected.

Section 4. The petition of the candidate shall be accompanied with the sum of two dollars which the Brother who presents the petition shall deposit in the hands of the Treasurer or be answerable for the same to the Lodge. This money shall be returned if the candidate is rejected and if received and initiated it shall be considered as part of his initiation fee.

Section 5. If a candidate after being balloted for and received fail to attend for initiation during three months unless from some unavoidable cause to be determined so by the Lodge at a stated meeting the deposit shall be forfeited to the lodge and the candidate considered otherwise upon the same footing as if he never had presented a petition.

Section 6. Any member or Brother who shall present a petition or second a motion for receiving it shall vouch the person to be one who he believes will conform to the rules of Masonry and will be of advantage to the Craft and the said member or brother shall also declare upon Masonic faith that they have no reason to believe that the initiation of the candidate would be disagreeable to any member or brother.

Section 7. Any brother being an ancient York Mason wishing to become a member of this Lodge must petition the same for that purpose and at the same time produce a certificate of his having paid all dues and arrearages to the Lodge of which he was last a member within the United States or give a satisfactory reason to the Lodge why he cannot produce the same and must be recommended by two Master Masons as is provided for candidates into the first degree of Masonry, after which he shall be balloted for, as in the case of balloting for a candidate and if admitted shall pay to the Treasurer the sum of Two Dollars if a Master Mason, Four Dollars if a Fellow Craft, and Six Dollars if but an Entered Apprentice.

Section 8. Every member of this Lodge who has been before a member of any other lodge and obtained a certificate from such Lodge shall deposit his certificate with the Secretary immediately on becoming a member of this Lodge or forfeit the sum of One Dollar for every month he detains it provided however that such certificate shall be returned to him whenever he withdraws from the Lodge.

Section 9. When a petition be presented for initiation every member shall be entitled to a vote.

ARTICLE VIII

Of Passing and Raising.

Section 1. Any brother wishing to be advanced shall produce a certificate from the Treasurer of his having paid all Lodge Dues and if time will permit he shall undergo an examination in open Lodge after which the propriety of advancing him to the proposed Degree shall be decided by a majority of the members present.

ARTICLE IX

Of the Payment.

Section 1. Every monthly member shall pay monthly into the Treasury the sum of fifty cents, every Quarterly member shall pay quarterly the sum of One Dollar, and every half yearly member shall pay half yearly the sum of One Dollar and Fifty Cents, except on the meetings when they attend when they shall pay the same as other members out of which sums the dues of the Grand Lodge and the expenses of the evening shall be paid provided the expenses of the evening shall in no case exceed the sum of twenty five cents for every member present and which shall be in full of their dues to the Grand Lodge and to the Lodge.

Section 2. The Fee for initiation shall be Ten Dollars, for passing Five, and the same for raising.

Section 3. The Tyler shall be entitled to demand from the Lodge One Dollar for his attendance each regular nights meeting, the sum of Two Dollars for every called Lodge to be paid by the brother or brethren for whose benefit the Lodge was called, and Three Dollars for his attendance on each of the Feast Days to be discharged out of the ordinary funds of the Initiation, also the sum of fifty cents from every new made brother and from every brother passed or raised which shall be in lieu of all his charges and shall moreover be exempt from all lodge contributions.

Section 4. No member who shall be in arrears for any sum more than six months shall be entitled to vote in any case whatever, or be eligible to any office in this lodge unless such arrearages be discharged.

Section 5. Should any brother be twelve months in arrears he shall be suspended from all the privileges of the

Order until such arrearages be paid unless such delinquencies arise from his necessary absence or some unavoidable accident to be adjudged of by the lodge.

ARTICLE X

Of the Funds of the Lodge.

Section 1. The Funds of the lodge shall consist of two separate and distinct heads.

Section 2. The Fees for Admission and for Degrees shall constitute the Charity Fund.

Section 3. The monthly quarterly and Semi-Annual contributions of the members and the sum paid for called Lodges shall contribute the funds for Current Expenses and for the payment of Dues to the Grand Lodge.

Section 4. The Treasurer pro tempore shall account for and pay to the Treasurer of the Lodge all monies by him received and shall also state the accounts of the members, who may have not paid their fees or contributions on the night when he was appointed pro tempore before the next meeting and in case of his failure shall stand charged with the whole amount of Fees and contributions due that meeting.

Section 5. A statement of the accounts so rendered and the sums paid shall be laid before the next state Lodge and upon order shall be entered on the Treasurer's account.

ARTICLE XI

Of Committees.

Section 1. All committees shall be appointed by the Worshipful Master or in his absence by the presiding Warden or Master pro tempore except when the Worshipful

Master shall be interested when the Senior Warden shall make the appointment.

Section 2. A standing committee shall be appointed after every annual Election to examine the Treasurers, Stewarts and other officers Books and accounts and shall report the situation thereof at each half yearly meeting before mentioned.

Section 3. The Worshipful Master and Wardens shall be a committee of Charity for the relief of transient Brethren or Strangers in distress to whom they shall advance out of the charity funds of the Lodge not exceeding Ten Dollars to each person at any one time and should the demands of the distressed person be for more than that sum they shall immediately call a Lodge and lay the subject before the Lodge and shall report their proceedings at each semi-annual meeting.

ARTICLE XII

Of Advancement.

Section 1. Every Brother who may wish to be passed or raised shall before he is advanced produce the Treasurer's Certificate.

ARTICLE XIII

Of Visiting Brethren.

Section 1. Any Brother wishing to visit this Lodge shall have his name announced by the Tyler and if not vouched for by at least two Master Mason members of this Lodge he shall be examined and if found to be an ancient York Mason shall be admitted as a visitor for the evening.

Section 2. As every Brother ought to be a member of some regular Lodge in the State, Territory, or County where he resides, no Brother resident in this Territory not being a member of any Lodge within the same shall be received as a visitor to this Lodge more than twice without being subject to the ordinary contribution.

Section 3. The second section of this Article is not to be considered as in any way applicable to Brethren, who are only sojourners in this Territory.

ARTICLE XIV

Of Withdrawing from the Lodge.

Section 1. Any member may withdraw himself from this Lodge on producing the Treasurers Receipt for all dues and giving Notice to the lodge. But no member shall be considered as having withdrawn himself without he has fully complied with this article.

ARTICLE XV

Of the Bye-Laws.

Section 1. A Master Mason who may wish to introduce a new Law or alter an existing one, shall hand up said Law or alteration in writing to the Master; after being perused by the Master it shall be read by the Secretary and if then seconded by a Master Mason it shall lie over one month and shall then be determined after a full discussion when concurrence of a majority of two-thirds of the members present shall be necessary to constitute it a part of those Laws.

Section 2. Every member shall be provided with a printed copy of the Bye-Laws at the expense of the Lodge.

Section 3. These Bye-Laws shall be entered by the Secretary in a Book to be procured for that purpose and every member on his admission into this Lodge shall subscribe these Laws thereby acknowledging himself bound in every respect strictly to comply with them.

Section 4. The former Bye-Laws of this Lodge is hereby repeated:

We the Committee report the above as the Bye-Laws of this Lodge.

(Here follows a list of the Members' Names.)

Supplement to the foregoing Bye-Laws.

At a regular meeting of Louisiana Lodge No. 109, October 12th, A.D. 1813, A.L. 5813. Notice was presented agreeable to the 1st Section of the 15th Article of our Bye-Laws for the alteration of the 1st section of the 1st article in said Bye-Laws.

When in conformity to said Notice on the 8th of November, 1813, being a regular Lodge night it was ordered by the Lodge that the said 1st section of the 1st article be as far repeated as respects the time of meeting and it shall read hereafter as follows:

The Lodge shall be convened on the first Monday night in every month and at such other times as the Worshipful Master, or the presiding Warden in his absence, shall judge proper.

Supplementary Supplement to the foregoing Bye-Laws.

At a regular meeting of Louisiana Lodge No. 109, April 3rd 1815, A.L. 5815, a notice was presented by Brother William Searcy for the alteration of the Supplement of our Bye-Laws passed on the 8th of November,

1813. Agreeable to the 1st Section of the 15th article of our Bye-Laws when in conformity to said notice on the first of May, 1815, being a regular Lodge night it was ordered that the above named Supplement passed on the 8th of November 1813 be hereby repeated and ordered also

That this lodge shall be convened on the second Monday night in every month and at such other times as the Worshipful Master, or the presiding Warden in his absence, shall think proper.

I, John Scott, Worshipful Master of Louisiana Lodge No. 109 held in the Town of St. Genevieve in the Missouri Territory under the authority of the Grand Lodge of Pennsylvania, do certify that the above and foregoing extra pages contains a correct and true copy of the Bye-Laws of the said lodge with the several amendments thereunto made from time to time and which collectively taken constitute the Bye-Laws of said Lodge under which we are governed.

In testimony whereof I have hereto set my hand the seal of said lodge to be appressed this 19th October 1815, Anno Lucis 5815.

JOHN SCOTT, *Master of Louisiana Lodge No.* 109.

Attest:
EDWD. ROBERTS, *Secretary.*

Bye-Laws of Lodge No. 109
Copy
of the Bye-Laws of Louisiana Lodge 109.

Read in G. L. 18th Dec. 1815 and referred to the Committee of Bye-Laws to examine and report thereon.

Committee reported 15th January 1816 and report adopted.

The report of this Committee is given in full:

To the R. W. *the Grand Lodge of Pennsylvania:*
The Committee on Bye-Laws to whom were referred the Bye-Laws of Lodge No. 109 held in the Town of St. Genevieve in the Missouri Territory, Respectfully Report

That they have carefully examined the same and recommend that they be adopted with the following exceptions and amendments to wit:

Article 1. In the first line strike out the words "and living."

Article 1, *Section* 4. Strike out this section.

Article 4, *Section* 2. Strike out "Secretary" and insert "Tyler."

Article 5, *Section* 2. Strike out this section.
    Section 3. Strike out this section.
    Section 5. Strike out this section.

Article 7, *Section* 1. Strike out all that follows "members of the Lodge" in the 9th line, until the words "the candidate" in the 17th line, and add the words "and qualifications" after the word "character" in the 19th line.

Article 7, *Section* 7. Strike out "ancient" in the first line and insert the words "being an ancient York" after the word "brother" in the same line.
    Section 9. Insert the words "be presented" after petition in the first line.

Article 8, *Section* 1. Strike out the word "ballot" and all that follows in the two last lines and insert "by a majority of the members present."

Article 9, *Section* 4. Strike out this section.

Article 13, *Section* 1. Insert "York" after "Ancient" in the sixth line.

Article 15, *Section* 1. Insert the word "after" in lieu of the word "upon" in the 8th line.
Strike out both amendments.
All of which is respectfully submitted.

    RICH BACHE
    GEORGE A. BAKER, Junior   } *Committee*
    NATN. R. POTTS

Phila., 4 January 1816.

The first return made by Louisiana Lodge to the Grand Lodge of Pennsylvania was for the year 1808; it is made on a printed form, evidently the standard form of the Grand Lodge;

I—Aaron Elliott—Worshipful Master of Lodge No. 109, Ancient York Masons held—at the Town of St. Genevieve, Territory of Louisiana—under the authority of the Right Worshipful Grand Lodge of Pennsylvania, do hereby Certify to the said Right Worshipful Grand Lodge; that at an election held this day, the following Brethren were duly elected officers of the said Lodge, for the term of twelve months, succeeding next St. John's Day: Viz,

    OTHO SHRADER, *Worshipful Master*
    HENRY DODGE, *Senior Warden*
    JOHN SCOTT, *Junior Warden*
    THOMAS OLIVER, *Secretary*
    EZEKIEL FENWICK, *Treasurer*

        In testimony whereof I have hereunto set my Hand, and caused the Seal of the said Lodge to be affixed at—St. Genevieve—the 12th—Day of—December—A. D. 18—08—

and in the year of Masonry 58—08—.

AARON ELLIOTT, *Master of Lodge No. 109—*

Attest:

THO. OLIVER, *Secretary of Lodge No. 109—*

A similar return was filed for the year ending December 1809, with the exception that the return was filled out by Brother Shrader, the Master during the year, who reports the following officers elected:

> OTHO SHRADER, *Worshipful Master*
> HENRY DODGE, *Senior Warden*
> JOHN SCOTT, *Junior Warden*
> SAMUEL H. T. YOUNG, *Secretary*
> JOHN McARTHUR, *Treasurer*

In each of the above returns the word "six months" has been stricken out and the words "twelve months" inserted, inferring that annual elections were held; in the latter certificate, the words "and caused the Seal of the said lodge to be affixed" has been erased and the words "and for want of a seal of said lodge, affix my private Seal" has been substituted.

The first return of members showed the following to have been charter members of No. 109:

BULLITT, GEORGE   MILLARD, JOSIAH
DODGE, HENRY   OLIVER, THOMAS
ELLIOTT, AARON   SCOTT, JOHN
HENRY, ANDREW   SHRADER, OTHO
HICKMAN, WILLIAM   TERRY, ROBERT
LASSOUS, LOUIS   VALLE, FRANCOIS
         SMITH, JOHN "T" (Fellowcraft)

The following initiations were reported. These men were first to receive degrees in the Territory:

KIMBALL, JOSEPH   May 9, 1808
SEARCY, WILLIAM   June 24, 1808
FENWICK, EZEKIEL   Sept. 12, 1808
DUNN, AZARIAH C.   Sept. 12, 1808

The second degree was conferred on the following:

KIMBALL, JOSEPH   May 11, 1808
SEARCY, WILLIAM   July 11, 1808
FENWICK, EZEKIEL   Oct. 18, 1808
DUNN, AZARIAH C.   Oct. 18, 1808

The third degree was also conferred during the year on the following:

SMITH, JOHN "T"   May 11, 1808
      (Admitted a member of this lodge on
      14th November 1808 being a Fellow-

craft of Lodge No. —— in the State of Tennessee.)

Kimball, Joseph	June 11, 1808
Searcy, William	Aug. 8, 1808
Fenwick, Ezekiel	Nov. 14, 1808
Dunn, Azariah C.	Nov. 14, 1808

The result of the year's work was to add five members by raising, and one (William Cabbeen, June 13, 1808) by affiliation, a total of eighteen members at the close of the year 1808, for none were lost by dimission, death or suspension.

The amount due the Grand Lodge of Pennsylvania, on the basis of the membership reported to the Grand Lodge, was $18.93, representing $1.00 per capita on each candidate initiated and 7c per month on each member. It was impossible to send the money with the returns, and it was not until May 27, 1809, that opportunity came to transmit the money to the Grand Secretary. The remittance was accompanied by the following letter:

Sir:

This covers a return of the members, an account of the last election of officers and also an amount of the dues to the Right Worshipful Grand Lodge of Pennsylvania, from Louisiana Lodge No. 109, which will be handed to you by Mr. William Shannon with the sum of Eighteen Dollars and 93 Cents.

This communication has been delayed in order to meet with a private and safe conveyance to Philadelphia. Whilst I apologize for giving you the trouble which is on account of our Lodge not having a person already chosen to transact their business, I must request the favor of you to receive the money from Mr. Shannon and procure your Treasurer's receipt for the amount.

      I am Sir
        Yr Mo Obt Servt
          THO OLIVER, *Secy.*

GEORGE A. BAKER, ESQ.
 Philadelphia.

The William Shannon referred to was the principal merchant in St. Genevieve in 1806. About 1810 we find him conducting a drug store (probably the first of its kind) in St. Louis, and it is very probable that his trip to Philadelphia was for the purchase of stock for his new business; Shannon later returned to St. Genevieve and represented that county in the last Territorial Legislature of 1818.

Shannon delivered the money and returns and took the receipt of the Grand Treasurer; the receipt reads:

July 5th, 1809. Received of Lodge No. 109, by the hands of Mr. William Shannon, Eighteen Dollars and Ninety Three Cents, Grand Lodge Dues of said Lodge up to the 27th December last, and for which I have given Duplicate Receipts.
$18.93.   JAMES L. BRADFORD, *G. Treasurer*
       Grand Lodge Penna.

The report for the year ending December 1809 showed the lodge to be active and progressive; two rejections were reported, John Calloway and Benjamin Strother. The total result of the year's work was shown in the thirty members on the rolls at the close of the year.

By initiation, passing and raising, there were added the names of Richard G. Bibb, J. B. Bossier, William Brown, John Donnahoe, J. B. Janis, John McArthur, Joseph Perkins, Henry Pinkley, John B. Regnier and Reuben Smith. (Regnier was affiliated as a Fellowcraft and then raised.)

By affiliation: Francois Regnier, Andrew Woods, Samuel H. T. Young.

By initiation only: Andrew Miller, Walter Wilkinson.

Losses: By expulsion, Joseph Kimball; by dimit, Ezekiel Fenwick, Azariah C. Dunn, William Brown.

The name of Nathaniel Cook appears on the 1809 report as a Master Mason; whether he was admitted by affiliation or by initiation is not known. The total during the year, thus tabulated, shows 34; losses 4; membership on December 27, 1809, 30. The amount of dues and per capita tax due the Grand Lodge this year amounted to $32.49, which was not remitted until March of the following year, for the reason explained in the following letter, written by Judge Otho Shrader, to the Grand Secretary:

>St. Genevieve, Terrt of
>Louisiana, March 1, 1810.

SIR AND BROTHER:

The bearer Brother Bartholomew Berthold of late a member of our Lodge, will deliver to you the sum of $32.49, being the amount of dues from said Lodge No. 109, to the R. W. Grand Lodge till the 27th Dec., last.—As we are under the necessity of forwarding these returns by mail, I have endeavoured to make them as light as possible in taking fine paper, and writing a small hand.—You will, I hope, pardon us for troubling you with presenting the returns and dues to the R. W. Grand Lodge.

I shall feel extremely gratified to hear of your and your familys' health and prosperity, and beg you to believe me sincerely,

>Your humble servant

GEORGE A. BAKER, ESQ.   OTHO SHRADER

Indorsed on the back of the paper is the notation of the Grand Secretary "Read in Grand Lodge 4 June 1810" and "For'd by Bartholomew Berthold, c/o Anthony Baber, Pittsburgh," inferring that Berthold went only as far east as Pittsburgh, although the official receipt of the Grand Treasurer reads:

Received June 2d, 1810, of Lodge No. 109, by the hands of Br. Bartholomew Berthold, thirty two dollars and fifty cents in full of Grand Lodge dues of said Lodge to December last and for which I have given duplicate receipts.

And then something happened, about which the record has little to say; no further report was made to the Grand Lodge until 1815. When John Scott became Master, and Edmund Roberts, Secretary, a Committee appointed by the lodge wrote the following explanatory letter:

     Sainte Genevieve, Missouri Territory.
     November 22, 1813.

SIR AND BROTHER:

 The undersigned a Committee appointed by Louisiana Lodge No. 109 at St. Genevieve beg leave through you to acknowledge to the Grand Lodge of Pennsylvania, that the Lodge is very sensible of the delay which has already taken place in not remitting the legal dues from hence to the Grand Lodge, and that this Lodge has no other apology to offer than difficulty in transmitting money to so great a distance. We are authorized to state that the Lodge will embrace the first convenient opportunity to remit the dues from hence, and in the meantime respectful ask a little further indulgence.

    We are Sir and Brother with great
     Esteem Yr Mo Ob Servts,
       THO. OLIVER
       W. SEARCY.

 Indorsed by Grand Secretary "Recd 27th Dec. 1813," "read in G. L. 27 Dec. 1813, and further time granted to the Lodge."

THE STORY OF LOUISIANA LODGE NO. 109

And finally, in June 1815, the returns for the years 1810, 1811, 1812, 1813, 1814 were made out and transmitted as if for one year. A tabulation of the returns shows that 7 members were added by affiliation, 27 by initiation, 1 Fellowcraft by affiliation, which with the 30 members of the last report, made a total number of members, 65. There were a few losses, however; 6 died, including Past Masters Aaron Elliott and Otho Shrader (which probably accounts for the unsettled condition of the lodge); 13 dimitted, leaving the total membership of No. 109, in June 1815, 46.

The complete list of officers of the lodge for the years 1808-15 is given below and is the last official report made to the Grand Lodge:

Year	Master	Sen. Warden	Jun. Warden
1808	Aaron Elliott	Andrew Henry	George Bullitt
1809	Otho Shrader	Henry Dodge	John Scott
1810	Otho Shrader	Henry Dodge	John Scott
1811	Otho Shrader	Henry Dodge	John Scott
1812	Henry Dodge	John Scott	J. B. Janis
1813	Henry Dodge	John Scott	J. B. Janis
1814	Henry Dodge	John Scott	J. B. Janis
1815	John Scott	Henry Keil	Th. Oliver

Year.	Sec'y.	Treas.
1809	Th. Oliver	E. Fenwick
1810	Saml. Young	J. McArthur
1811	Wm. Searcy	J. McArthur
1812	Wm. Searcy	J. McArthur
1813	Andrew Scott	J. McArthur
1814	Henry Keil	Jos. Hertick
1815	Edm. Roberts	Th. T. Iong

February 3, 1816, the Grand Treasurer acknowledged receipt of $203.32 from Brother Henry Keil, S. W. of Louisiana Lodge No. 109, the last payment known to have been made to the Mother Grand Lodge. This was the period of Grand Lodges; several neighboring States had organized Grand Lodges, and Tennessee, just across the river, was giving out charters right and left on request. Members of the lodge at St. Louis had forfeited their Pennsylvania charter and taken one from Tennessee; members at Herculaneum and St. Charles had sought dispensations from the new Grand Lodge; and then, in 1821, Missouri organized her own Grand Lodge, and it is very probable St. Genevieve received an invitation to become a member.

How could Louisiana Lodge get away from the Grand Lodge of Pennsylvania in a gracious manner, particularly when indebted to them for several years' dues? That was the question which concerned them. And so they did nothing.

Then came, as always comes, a day of reckoning; St. Genevieve wanted to join the Grand Lodge of Missouri; how could that be done, when it was necessary for each of the members to show himself in good Masonic standing? Brother Henry Keil, a former Master of No.

109, took upon himself the burden of the communication with the Grand Lodge, and his correspondence brings out many things not mentioned in the returns.

To the Most Worshipful, the *Grand Lodge of Pennsylvania:—*

The Subscribers, Master Masons, and members of Louisiana Lodge No. 109, have learned with deep regret, by a letter dated in November last, from the Grand Secretary of the Most Worshipful Grand Lodge of Pennsylvania, that they have been suspended from the rights and privileges of the fraternity, by reason of the non-payment of dues from the Lodge of which we are members to the M. W. the Grand Lodge of Penna.

That the Louisiana Lodge No. 109 may have been culpably negligent with regard to her communications and payment of dues to the Grand Lodge, we are however reluctantly obliged to admit; but as members of the former Lodge, we must, in justice to ourselves, declare that individually, we ever have been and now are ready to meet our full proportion of all delinquent dues; and we humbly pray of the M. W. Grand Lodge, that some person may be duly authorized to receive from us our proportion of the aforesaid, and that we may be restored to those rights and benefits, from which we now stand suspended.

Should the Grand Lodge prefer such a course, we are ready and willing to remit our several individual dues to the proper officers, by mail or otherwise, without the intervention of an agent, on the part of the M. W. G. Lodge.

Praying the Most Worshipful Grand Lodge to give our

case an early and favorable consideration, we are, with sentiments of the highest respect,

    The M. W. G. Lodges' Most Ob Servants
                  JOHN OKLASS
                  JAMES CLARK
                  NICHOLAS FLEMING
St. Genevieve, Missouri THO. OLIVER
    April 4, 1825.   SEBASTIAN BURTSCHER

On the same petition was the statement from Brother Keil:

I, Henry Keil, Certify that I have been a member of Louisiana Lodge No. 109, and that I withdrew on the 7th of May 1821, by the consent of the Lodge, on account of my Avocation of Life.

In the winter of 1815-1816 I had the honor of setting as a Member of the Most Worshipful Grand Lodge of Pennsylvania being then Senior Warden of Sd Louisiana Lodge and paid dues of Sd Lodge to the Grand Secretary, Brother Joseph G. Lewis.

I further certify that Sebastian Burtscher of late Louisiana Lodge was initiated and became a member of late L. L. No. 109 while I was a member of Sd Lodge, after my return from Philadelphia, on the 10th of June 1816, and that John Oklass and James Clark were initiated and became members of Sd late Lodge on the 26th day of Dec. 1821, and Nicholas Fleming was also initiated and became a member about the same time, the precise day I do not recollect, but the three latter Gentlemen were made Masons in my presence, while I was a visitor to Sd L. L. No. 109.

Thomas Oliver's name is to be found on the return I took with me from Louisiana Lodge to the M. W. Grand

THE STORY OF LOUISIANA LODGE NO. 109

Lodge at the time above mentioned, and deposited the same there.

At the request of those five gentlemen, M. M. and Members of Sd late Louisiana Lodge, I have given this Certificate.

Ste. Genevieve, Missouri, May the 5th day 1825.
HENRY KEIL, M. M.
and former member of
Louisiana Lodge No. 109.

The charter had been ordered, vacated, and forfeited June 7, 1824; on receipt of Brother Keil's letter, the matter was placed in the hands of the Grand Master. From Brother Keil's letter, we judge that he was authorized to do what he could to adjust the financial affairs of the lodge; his letter to the Grand Secretary under date of November 30, 1825, says:

I duly received your favor of June 28th last, in which you inform me the Right Worshipful G. Master of the Grand Lodge of Pennsylvania requests and authorizes me to settle the affairs of the late Louisiana Lodge No. 109, which I have from Masonic Motives and zeal for the Interests of the fraternity undertaken to perform. Some of the Members of the late Lodge No. 109, having requested a Brother M. M. not a member of that Lodge to assist me in drawing off and arranging the accounts, we have proceeded to perform that duty with all the promptitude consistent with our usual Avocation. You will hence perceive that the books are in my possession. The furniture, Jewels,

Etc., have also been delivered to me, and they will be disposed of and the proceeds remitted together with such other sums as I may receive from members agreeably to your Instructions. Should no private opportunity offer for forwarding the Charter within a short time, I shall forward it to you by mail. I regret the very important business trusted to me has been delayed so long. My apology rests in the labour I have been obliged to perform in extracting the accounts from a ten years record. And now that accounts are prepared for a settlement, I feel it my duty to the members of the late Lodge No. 109 to state, that if a little longer delay should take place in making that settlement, their scattered Situation may perhaps be pleaded in Excuse, as few of them, now live within 30 or 40 or 50 miles of this place. To give you an idea, in one word, of their state of dispersion, one member and two frequent visitors of this Lodge, have recently returned from beyond the Rocky Mountains.

A number of members of the late Lodge No. 109 have expressed a wish to me, to desire the R. W. Grand Lodge, through your Medium to look at them with the Eye of Charity; that they have tried to keep the Lodge up that they could not form a Lodge since July 1822 (the last meeting of the Lodge) and that they are willing to pay up their Grand Lodge dues to November 1824, the time of their suspension, and that they are prepared to pay their shares in discharging the Debts owing to divers persons by the late Lodge—and wish to be reinstated. I hope you will honor me with an answer, after the half yearly meeting on the 27th Dec. etc.

I remain Yours fraternally,
HENRY KEIL
Formerly of Lodge No. 109.

THE STORY OF LOUISIANA LODGE NO. 109

Within a month after writing the last letter, Brother Keil wrote again to the Grand Secretary:

In my last letter of November 30th, I mentioned to you, that I would forward the Charter of the late Louisiana Lodge No. 109, by mail, if no private opportunity should offer.

Since that, Mr. E. F. Pratte, merchant of this town, has concluded going on to Philadelphia and promised me to take a letter for me. I therefore send you the above mentioned Charter, hereby enclosed, hoping it may come safely to your hands.

Sometime later, November 29, 1826, additional members of the lodge took up the matter with the Grand Lodge as is shown by the following letter and petition:

The petition of the undersigned, Master Masons, respectfully shows, That we were members of Louisiana Lodge No. 109, at the time the charter of that Lodge was recalled by the R. W. Grand Lodge in the year 1824—That some time since we petitioned the R. W. Grand Lodge, setting forth our peculiar situation, and praying for relief—That in compliance with our petition, the R. W. Grand Lodge empowered W. Henry Keil of this place as Agent of the Grand Lodge, to settle the Accounts of the members and generally to close the business of our Lodge.

We would, however, respectfully represent, that the plan for closing our business, adopted by the Grand Lodge at our former request, has failed of success owing to the very limited scope of the instructions given by the Grand Lodge to its agent here; those instructions, it is conceived, not authorizing him to settle the account of any individual or any other principle than by the payment to him of amounts prima facie due on the books of the Lodge. Whereas, some of us have claims against our Lodge which would partly pay the amount which stands against us, and some of us have claims which, if liquidated, would leave a balance in our favor. We would further represent that it now is and has ever been our wish to comply with all the requirements of Masonry, while at the same time, our situation in life is such that we are unable consistently, with the duties we owe to ourselves and family, to pay all the dues which appear against us, unless our claims should be allowed. For these reasons as well as for various others which will suggest themselves to the minds of the members of the R. W. Grand Lodge, we pray, that our Charter may be returned to us for the purpose of closing our business, in the same manner as has been granted to our friends and neighbors of Western Star Lodge No. 107.

>Lewis Linn
>H. Dodge
>Nicholas Fleming
>James Clark
>John Oklass
>S. Burtscher
>D. P. Etter
>G. A. Bird

While this correspondence was being carried on with the Grand Lodge of Pennsylvania, the brothers of St. Genevieve were arranging with the new Grand Lodge of Missouri for a charter. One month before the above letter was written, they received a charter from the Grand Lodge of Missouri, authorizing them to carry on the work of a lodge at St. Genevieve under the name of Tucker Lodge No. 13, the membership, no doubt, being somewhat dubious about retaining the name Louisiana under the circumstances. The charter for the new lodge was dated October 10, 1826.

Brother Keil continued his efforts to settle the affair with the Grand Lodge of Pennsylvania, but with little success; he wrote the Grand Lodge under date of April 24, 1827:

In compliance with the Instructions contained in the Communication of the Grand Secy. made to me; I proceeded to take possession of the Jewels, Furniture and etc. of Louisiana Lodge No. 109, which in a former letter I mentioned to the Grand Secretary.

With the assistance of a Masonic Brother, not a member of that Lodge, in the most Correct manner arranged the accounts of the Lodge, and called on the members for a settlement of their several dues. This Settlement has been made in one or two instances, where the dues were very trifling, but the members generally decline to pay the balances which appear against them, principally on the following grounds;

First:—By the minutes of the late Lodge, it appears, that the monthly dues were, at a particular time, by resolution of the Lodge, raised, from 50c to $1 pr month, and there is no record to show that this resolution ever was rescinded; but the members universally assert that this resolution *was* rescinded a short time after, and I think it very hard that they should be obliged to pay for the neglect of their Secretary in not recording this abrogation.

Second:—Many of the members have accounts and other claims against this late Lodge, which, although never presented and allowed by the Lodge, yet, which as they contend, are just and true and would be allowed by the Lodge, were it yet authorized to work. Some of these claims would overbalance the dues of those holding them, and others would, if allowed, lighten the burden of an unliquidated balance. With regards to the first plea assigned for a non-settlement of the accounts, I will remark, that I have occasion to believe it well founded.

First, from the uniform aspersion of the members of the late Lodge.

Second, From the settlements of some of the accounts on the books by the late Secretary (now unfortunately deceased) where the dues, excepting for a very short period appear to have been Calculated at 50 cents per month, and accruing after the passage of the resolved raising the dues to $1 pr month, and

Third—From a resolution found among the loose papers of the Lodge (but without date) for the reduction of the dues to the original sum of 50c pr month.

Respecting the second plea, above stated, permit me to remark that I have every reason to believe it (generally speaking) to be entitled to consideration, from many of the Circumstances on which the Claims are founded from my own knowledge.

After much reflection, I have come to the conclusion that however well founded may be the reasons of members for declining a settlement of their dues, as they appear on the Books, yet that the remedy was beyond the powers entrusted to me. Under these circumstances, my Council to those concerned was, they should petition the R. W. G. Lodge for the return of their Charter for the settlement of their concerns, as I was informed had been done by our Neighbors of Western Star Lodge No. 107.

I was informed that such of the members, as were here at the time, did so petition the R. W. G. Lodge, but that no reply had as yet been received by them. Should the R. W. G. Lodge think proper to grant their prayer, I have no doubt that from the character of the members generally, their business will be closed with the greatest possible promptitude.

The Charter of Louisiana Lodge No. 109, I forwarded on, to the Grand Secretary under date of Dec. 4, 1825, by Mr. E. F. Pratte of this place, who informed me that he delivered it to a certain Gentleman by the name of Brazier, who I think I sat with in Lodge No. 73. I never received any acknowledgment of its receipt, but presume it must have arrived safe to hand.

I remain yours fraternally,

HENRY KEIL.

But one other paper remains to bear witness to the further efforts of the old lodge to settle its troubles; this is a letter from the Grand Secretary of the Grand Lodge of Missouri, John D. Daggett, to the Grand Secretary of the Grand Lodge of Pennsylvania: (the date is October 8, 1828):

The communication received from the Gr. Secy. of the Gr. Lodge of Pennsylvania relating to Louisiana Lodge

No. 109 having been duly considered, the following resolution was unanimously adopted, viz:

Resolved that this Grand Lodge will freely acquiesce in the revival of Louisiana Lodge No. 109, at St. Genevieve by the Grand Lodge of Pennsylvania for the purpose of collecting its debts and closing its business.

No record is known of further action by the Grand Lodge of Pennsylvania in the matter of reviving No. 109. The brethren were enjoying their Masonic membership in Tucker Lodge No. 13, and there was no immediate reason why they should pay several years' back dues, when the amounts were in question and when some of their legitimate claims had not been allowed. Legally, they were probably indebted to their old Grand Lodge, but there were certain moral rights which entitled them to some consideration; even our old friend and brother, Henry Keil, whose advice seemed most timely, sympathised with his less fortunate brethren who had remained with the lodge until it was thrown on the rocks of lethargy.

How these brethren ever received dimits and applied to other lodges for affiliation (or in some cases as charter members of new lodges), it is impossible to state, but there is ample evidence that they did. We suspect that some of the new lodges were not very insistent on legal requirements under such circumstances.

THE STORY OF LOUISIANA LODGE NO. 109

We have told the story of this lodge somewhat beyond the Territorial period, because it was a Territorial Lodge, and because it never (as No. 109) became a member of the Grand Lodge in the Territory. As Tucker Lodge No. 13, it began its history anew, acknowledging allegiance to the Grand Lodge of Missouri; its history as No. 13 is reserved for another time.

Thus ends the story of the first lodge west of the Mississippi River after an existence of almost twenty years; it was a light shining in the wilderness, a beacon for the Masonic pioneer. Around its rude Altar gathered men of many faiths, both Protestant and Catholic; the spirit of bigotry and intolerance had not reached St. Genevieve at that time. Men engaged in pioneering had strong need for an organization which exemplified brotherhood, for a society which afforded opportunity for men of ideals to assemble together, man to man, and a chance to get away from their daily avocations. As such, Louisiana Lodge No. 109 fulfilled their most ardent desires.

What lodge to-day can boast of such a distinguished line of active members, as did Louisiana, with Senators Scott and Linn, General Dodge, Captain Shrader, Andrew Henry, Andrew Scott, George Bullitt and a host of others, good men and true, who blazed the trail of Freemasonry through the Mississippi Valley?

Such men deserve to have their names placed on perpetual record among the archives of the fraternity; we accordingly list the following members as shown by the returns of Louisiana Lodge No. 109, during its fifth of a century existence:

Austin, Stephen F.

Bullitt, George; (C) P. M.
Bossier, John B.
Bird, G. A.
Bibb, Richard G.
Berthold, Bartholomew
Bates, William
Brady, James G; P. M.
Brown, Robert T.
Burtscher, Sebastian

Cabbeen, William; P. M.

Cook, Nathaniel
Crittenden, T. T.
Cheatham, Edward
Craighead, Alexander
Clark, James

Dodge, Josiah
Daggett, Peter

Dodge, Henry C; (C); P. M.
Dunn, Azariah
Donnahoe, John; P. M.
Dowlin, James

Elliott, Aaron; (C); P. M.
Elliott, Charles
Elliott, Elias A; P. M.
Elliott, Henry; P. M.
Etter, D. P.

Fenwick, Ezekiel
Fleming, Nicholas

Gouion, John J.

Henry, Andrew (C)
Hickman, William (C)
Hertick, Joseph
Hubbard, Simon M.

Iong, Theodore F; P. M.
Janis, John Bte; P. M.
Jones, John; P. M.

Kimball, Joseph
Keil, Henry; P. M.

Lassous, Louis (C)
Lane, Harvey
Linn, Lewis F.

Martin, James
Millard, Josiah; (C); P. M.
McArthur, John; P. M.
Miller, Andrew
McGrady, Israel
McClenahan, Josiah

Oliver, Thomas (C)
Oklass, John

Perkins, Joseph
Pettit, Jacob
Pinkley, Henry
Pusey, Nathan; P. M.

Regnier, Francois
Roe, Daniel
Roberts, Edmund; P. M.
Robertson, John H.

Shrader, Otho; (C); P. M.
Scott, John; (C); P. M.
Smith, John "T"; (C as Fct)
Searcy, William; P. M.
Smith, Reuben
Scott, Andrew

Terry, Robert; (C)

Valle, Francois; (C)
Varner, William

Wilkinson, Walter
Weber, John H.
Wood, James
Welch, Thomas M.
Wilson, Nicholas; P. M.
Whitlow, Coleman

Young, Samuel H. T.

(C) charter member November 14, 1807; (P. M.) Past Master.

CHAPTER IX

THE LODGE OF MERIWETHER LEWIS

ST. LOUIS Lodge No. 111 was not the oldest west of the Mississippi River, but it was a remarkable one, for among its members were two of the Territorial Governors of Louisiana, and two Governors of the State of Missouri, the first Grand Master of Missouri, and the first Royal Arch Mason west of the Mississippi River.

St. Louis, in 1808, was not the most fertile field which might have been found in which to locate a lodge of Freemasons, and, but for the influence of the Governor of the Territory, it might never have been organized. In Meriwether Lewis, fresh from his conquest of the West, Freemasonry found an active exemplar. Such a strong character had no trouble in associating with him such men as Riddick, Garnier, Chouteau, Kimball, Easton, Bruff and other influential members of the fraternity.

THE LODGE OF MERIWETHER LEWIS

At an informal meeting held in the quarters of General Lewis, the need for a lodge in which brethren of the Mystic Tie might assemble around a common Altar was discussed. The meeting drew up and signed the following application for dispensation, to submit to the Grand Lodge of Pennsylvania:

To the Right Worshipful Grand Lodge of Pennsylvania:
The undersigned now are or have been members of regular Lodges, and having the good of the fraternity at heart, we are willing to exert our best endeavors to promote and diffuse the genuine principles of Masonry; that for the conveniency of our respective dwellings and for other good reasons, we are desirous of forming a new Lodge, in the town of St. Louis, in the Territory of Louisiana, to be named and styled Saint Louis Lodge—we therefore pray for a warrant of constitution to empower us to assemble as a legal lodge, to discharge the duties of Masonry in a regular and constitutional manner, according to the original form of the Order and the regulations of your Grand Lodge.

We have nominated and do recommend his Excellency Meriwether Lewis, a Past Master, to be the first Master; Thomas Fiveash Riddick to be the first Senior Warden and Rufus Easton to be the first Junior Warden of the said Lodge.

If the prayer of our petition should be granted, we promise strict conformity to all the constitutional laws and regulations of your Grand Lodge.

Be pleased to accept our Brotherly salutations.

Given under our hands at St. Louis the 2d day of August A. L. 5808.

                                      MERIWETHER LEWIS
                                      THOS. F. RIDDICK, *Master*
                                        J. V. GARNIER
JOHN HAY, *Master*
JOHN HAYS, *Master*   JOSEPH KIMBALL, *Master*
MICHL. IMMELL, *Master* RUFUS EASTON, *Master*
                                        B. WILKINSON (*Appr*)
                                        J. BRUFF, *Royal Arch*
                                        JOHN COONS, *Master.*

Masonic law then, as now, required the approval of the nearest lodge, which in this case was Louisiana Lodge No. 109, at St. Genevieve. Within six days, the proposed application was submitted to the lodge sixty miles away, and their approval gained, in the following certificate signed by the first Master, Dr. Aaron Elliott.

We, the Worshipful Master, Wardens and Members of the Louisiana Lodge No. 109, holden in the City of St. Genevieve,

Do by these presents recommend to the Right Worshipful Grand Lodge of Pennsylvania those brethren whose names are to the foregoing petition as regular Masons, and we do further recommend Brother Meriwether Lewis as a Past Master Mason, Thomas Fiveash Riddick, a Master Mason, and Brother Rufus Easton, a Master Mason, as proper persons to fill the respective offices to which they have been nominated in a new Lodge to be constituted in the town of St. Louis under the Jurisdiction of the Right Worshipful Grand Lodge of Pennsylvania.

In testimony whereof we have hereunto set our hands and for want of a public seal annex our private seals in open lodge this eighth day of August 1808, and of Masonry 5808.

   Seal.
Tho. Oliver, *Secretary.*

     Aaron Elliott, *M.*
     John Scott, *Sen. Warden Pro tem.*
     Geo. Bullitt, *Jr. W.*

The entire burden of correspondence between the Grand Lodge of Pennsylvania and the proposed lodge was carried on by Judge Otho Shrader, active in the formation of Louisiana Lodge, and himself, at one time, a member of a Pennsylvania lodge. The application for dispension, together with its approval by Louisiana Lodge, must have been rushed, through the mediation of General Lewis, because we find its receipt acknowledged in a letter from the Grand Master thirty-three days later.

Dear Sir & Brother,
 I enclose you an application for a warrant which I received in a letter this day from our worthy and indefatigable brother, Judge Otho Shrader.

You will observe that His Excellency Governor Lewis is the proposed Master, & I understand the Brethren united with him are respectable.

Mr. Shrader mentions that Governor Lewis leaves St. Louis early in November, on a journey to the Atlantic States; so that I fear, considering the distance and the time it may take them after receiving the Warrant to complete the organization of the Lodge, our adjourned meeting will be rather late for the business.

If therefore you perceive no material impediment in the way of an Extra G. Lodge, I would therefore thank you to issue notices for the same on the first *vacant* night.

Ever faithfully yours,
James Milnor, G. M.

Br. G. A. Baker, M. W. G. S.   Sep. 10, 1808.

P.S. I called on you but had not the pleasure of meeting with you at home.

Meriwether Lewis was a name to conjure with, and no time was lost by the Most Worshipful Grand Lodge; six days after the above letter was written, the much desired warrant was on its way to its destination, where the little band of eleven Master Masons waited to receive it.

The warrant was addressed to Judge Shrader who was charged with the duty of constituting; it was not until November 8, 1808, almost two months following its issue, that the lodge was set at work. The warrant reads:

THE LODGE OF MERIWETHER LEWIS

WE, JAMES MILNOR, Esquire, Right Worshipful Grand Master of Masons in and for the Commonwealth of Pennsylvania and Masonic Jurisdiction thereunto belonging.

To our Worthy and Much Respected Brother Otho Shrader, Esquire, a Past Master Mason

GREETING:—

Reposing the greatest confidence in your Zeal, Fervor, and Constancy in the Craft, WE DO by virtue of the Powers and Authorities in US vested hereby authorize and empower you to call to your assistance a sufficient number of known and approved Past Master Masons to open and Constitute a New Lodge to be held at the Town of St. Louis in the Territory of Louisiana in the United States of America. And there to proceed to the Installation of Our Worthy and much Respected Brother Meriwether Lewis, Esquire, Master Elect and other the officers of a New Lodge there to be established and Constituted to be named and styled "Saint Louis Lodge" Number One Hundred and Eleven according to the most Ancient and Honourable Custom of the Royal Craft in all ages and amongst all Nations throughout the Known World and not contrarywise and make report to us hereon endorsed of your proceedings.

This Dispensation to remain in force for Six Months from the Date hereof and no longer.

Given under Our Hand and the Seal of Our Right Worshipful Grand Lodge at the City of Philadelphia in the said Commonwealth of Pennsylvania this Sixteenth Day of September in the year of Our

TERRITORIAL MASONRY

Lord 1808 and of MASONRY 5808.

Attest:
GEORGE A. BAKER,   JAMES MILNOR.
   Grand Secretary.

Shrader made a trip to St. Louis, constituted the lodge and filed the following Certificate with the Grand Secretary:

TO JAMES MILNOR, ESQUIRE,
   Right Worshipful Grand Master in and for the Commonwealth of Pennsylvania and Masonic Jurisdiction thereunto belonging,
   I do hereby certify that in pursuance of the within Dispensation to me directed, having called to my assistance a sufficient number of Past Master Masons, I have on Tuesday the eighth of November instant constituted and opened at the Town of St. Louis in the Territory of Louisiana, in the United States of America, Lodge Number One Hundred & Eleven and have installed our worthy and much respected Brother Meriwether Lewis, Esq., Master, and other the officers of the said Lodge styled St. Louis Lodge No. 111, according to the Ancient and most honourable custom of the Royal Craft.
   In testimony whereof I have hereunto set my hand at the Town of St. Louis aforesaid this eighth day of November in the year of our Lord 1808, and of Masonry 5808.
                                                OTHO SHRADER.

Shrader was just an ordinary backwoods Judge, but he handled Masonic titles and forms in a way which must have gladdened even the hearts of the M. W. Grand Lodge of the Keystone State.

Masonic lodges of 1808 in Louisiana Territory did not meet in "Temples." The Temple of Louisiana Lodge was an old French house of upright timbers, erected by Jacques Denis, the joiner, in 1765, to house the village pool hall. It was occupied as such during all of the Spanish régime. In dimensions the building was 20 x 40 feet, situated on the east side of Second Street next below Walnut. No. 111 resorted to no "drives," engaged in no lotteries, and sold neither punch boards nor prizes, and yet the leading men of the community were attracted to their "Temple" which was once a pool hall.

Unfortunately, No. 111 made no report to the Grand Lodge of its activity; its records were either lost, burned or destroyed, and its history must be gleaned from other sources. The Feast Days of St. John the Baptist were celebrated on at least two occasions, once in 1809, previous to the death of Meriwether Lewis, and the other, on the year following his death. Notices of the celebration appeared in the Louisiana Gazette at the time:

> The St. Louis Lodge No. 111, will celebrate the festival of St. John the Baptist on Saturday, the 24th instant, at

their Lodge room in St. Louis. Such Brethren (not members of the Lodge) as may wish to join in the celebration of this festival are requested to attend.

The procession will form at the Lodge room at twelve o'clock precisely, and march from thence to the church, where a Masonic oration will be delivered by a brother.

Dinner on the table at three o'clock.

By order of the Lodge.

June 20, 1809.   JOSEPH V. GARNIER, *Secretary*.

Two years later a similar notice appeared in the Louisiana Gazette:

Monday, the 24th inst., being the festival of St. John the Baptist, such Brethren (not members of the Lodge) as are desirous to celebrate the above festival are notified that St. Louis Lodge No. 111, will assemble at their room in the morning of said day, and march from thence to Brother Christy's, where a dinner will be provided for them.

June 11, 1811.   ALEXANDER MCNAIR
JEREMIAH CONNOR
JOSEPH V. GARNIER
Committee of Arrangements.

The Alexander McNair referred to was the first Governor of Missouri; Jeremiah Connor was Sheriff, and Joseph Garnier was Clerk of the Supreme Court and all active, Masonically.

In the same year, 1811, the lodge observed the anniversary of St. John the Evangelist, the occasion being marked by the singing of a Masonic ode expressly composed for the occa-

THE LODGE OF MERIWETHER LEWIS

sion by Lieut. Joseph Cross of the U. S. Artillery, stationed at the military barracks; the ode was printed in full in the local newspaper. Cross was born in 1777 and entered the army in 1797; he came to St. Louis in 1810, with troops destined for Ft. Bellefontaine. He was then sent to Natchez, Miss., where troops were being concentrated for the taking of Baton Rouge, then held by the Spanish. He returned East by water, returning to St. Louis in 1811, attending many of the meetings of No. 111 as a visitor.

It is most unfortunate that such scant records of this lodge remain; some day its original record book may be discovered; if so, it will be a priceless discovery, containing as it does the action of a small but noted group who were primarily responsible for the introduction of Freemasonry in Louisiana Territory.

It would be unfair to him who served this lodge as its first Master, and whose personality had so much to do with placing Masonry on a high level in St. Louis, not to speak of the sad end which came to our friend and brother, Meriwether Lewis.

In 1809, Governor Lewis, having business with the government at Washington, made the trip overland by way of the "Natchez Trace." This necessitated his going down the Mississippi River as far as the present site of

Memphis, and from there following a clearing made through the wood, known as the "Natchez Trace." Taking with him only a few servants, he began his journey. At about a day's journey west of Newburgh, Lewis County, Tennessee, he determined to spend the night; from this time on we do not know what happened. The family at whose home he spent the night told that their guest committed suicide, which for a time was generally accepted. But developments of a later date lead us to believe that he was foully murdered in the expectancy of securing money. It is not proper here to recount the harrowing details of the last hours of his life; rather would we call attention to the recognition taken by the legislature of the State in which he spent his dying hours.

December 21, 1843, the Tennessee Legislature passed an act, creating the county of Lewis from four other counties, so that his remains lie in the exact center of the county; February 4, 1848, the same Legislature appropriated $500 for the erection of a suitable monument.

The monument as it now stands is twenty and a half feet high; the design is simple, but intended to express the difficulties, successes and violent termination of a life marked by bold enterprise, manly courage and devoted patriotism. The base is of rough unhewn stone, eight feet high and nine feet square; on this rests a plinth, four feet square and eighteen inches in thickness on which are the inscriptions. On the plinth stands a broken column, eleven feet in height, denoting his untimely death, stricken down in the performance of duty.

The inscriptions read:

MERIWETHER LEWIS

Born near Charlottesville, Virginia
August 18, 1774
Died October 11, 1809, aged 35 years.

An officer of the Regular Army; Commander of the expedition to the Oregon in 1803-06. Governor of the Territory of Louisiana; his melancholy death occurred where this monument now stands, and under which his mortal remains rest.

Equally as prominent in the life of the Territory (and later the State) was General William Clark; Clark was one of the initiates of St. Louis No. 111, as his diploma will testify:

WISDOM! STRENGTH! FRATERNITY!
To all lawful and regularly constituted Lodges, and all lawful Brethren on the face of the Globe.
We, the Master and Wardens of Saint Louis Lodge Number One Hundred and Eleven, Ancient York Masons, held at Saint Louis in the Territory of Louisiana, by virtue

of a regular Warrant from the Worshipful, the Grand Lodge of the Commonwealth of Pennsylvania.

Send Greeting.

This is to certify that—William Clark—who has signed his name in the Margin, and unto whom we grant these letters, is a regular and registered Master Mason, entered, passed and raised in our said Lodge; and that he has performed all his works amongst us to the entire satisfaction of our said Lodge.

We therefore pray all duly constituted Lodges and all Free and Accepted Masons to receive him in fellowship, wheresoever he may be found.

IN TESTIMONY WHEREOF, We have hereunto set our hands and caused the same to be attested by our Secretary.

Done at Saint Louis the—eighteenth—day of—September—A.D.—one thousand eight hundred and nine—and of Masonry five thousand eight hundred and nine.

FREDERICK BATES,
Master
THOS. F. RIDDICK,
Senior Warden
JOHN COONS,
Junior Warden

Attest:
J. V. GARNIER,
Secretary.

It is interesting to note that Clark's diploma was issued *after* the departure of Lewis for Washington and within a few days of his untimely death in Tennessee.

No record appears in the records of Missouri

No. 1 of St. Louis as to Clark's membership in that lodge; it is very probable that he never affiliated, the old theory of "Once a Mason, always a Mason" being almost a landmark at the time, and yet, on the occasion of his death, September 1, 1838, an emergent communication of St. Louis Lodge No. 20, successor of Missouri No. 1, was called and the following proceedings were had:

Sunday morning, September 2, A.D. 1838, A.L. 5838.
   The Lodge was called on account of the death of our worthy brother, Genl. William Clark—
   Present, A. B. CHAMBERS, *W. M.*
       EDWARD KLINE, *S. W.*
       G. H. C. MELODY, *Treas.*
       RICHD. B. DALLAM, *Secy.*
       GEORGE WILSON, *S. D. pro tem*
       D. F. LEE, *J. D. pro tem*
       T. ANDREWS, *Tyler pro tem*
       BROTHERS MAGUIRE, JACKARD *and* MATHIAS.
   Opened a Masters Lodge.
   A motion was made to appoint a committee to confer with the friends of our decd brother Genl. Clark, to make arrangements for his interment in Masonic Order.
   Brothers Andrews, Little and Lee appointed that Comtee.
   The Lodge adjourned to meet this evening at seven o'clock.

The lodge met again the same evening with many more members present, and news of his death having been spread rapidly; in addition to those present at the morning session, there were: Joseph Foster, Jesse Little, James Magehan, Esrom Owens, Bernard Pratte, Bosworth, Dr. Ragan (Potomac No. 5, D. C.), Amos Evans (Lodge 39, Albany, Ind.), Failor (Indiana No. 39), J. C. Laveille, and Stephen Price from Concord Lodge, Baltimore, Md.

Lodge was opened in the third degree and *a degree conferred*, after which,

On motion, Brothers Pratte and Andrews were appointed Marshals to superintend a procession to be had on to-morrow for the purpose of interring our deed Brother Genl. W. Clark in Masonic Order, and all Brethren were requested to attend. Lodge was adjourned to meet tomorrow morning, Monday, half past eight o'clock.

At the appointed hour they met, when A. B. Chambers, later Grand Master of the Grand Lodge of Missouri, presided as Master and opened the lodge in the third degree. There were present on this occasion, what was at that time regarded as a large representation of Masons (this was the year when the anti-masonic feeling had almost exhausted itself). There were present, in addition to W. Bro. Chambers, S. V. Fransworth, Edward Kline, G. H. C. Melody, Richard B. Dallam, Clark Hooper, James Magehan, Esrom Owens, George Wilson, Bernard Pratte, Maguire,

Mathias, Louis Jackard, Hull, Papin, Dewitt, Andrews, Morton, Shaw, McKee, Williams, West, Barry, Norton, E. H. Shepherd, Fallon, Bosworth, Mills, Joseph Foster, Recordon, Singleton, Disbrow, Scott and Cleland, John Daggett, Masure, Brishta, Derham, and Dr. C. C. Campbell.

The remainder of the record tells the simple story of the final interment of all that was mortal of one whose name was a household word over a quarter of a century previous:

> Our deceased Brother William Clark was born on the first day of August 1770, and died on the first day of September, 1838, aged sixty eight years & 1 month.
> A procession was formed and proceeded to the house where the corpse of our decd Brother Clark was, and from thence to the place of interment and deposited the same in Masonic order in ancient and solemn form, after which they returned to the Lodge and the following Resolutions were offered and adopted—Resolved that the members of this Lodge wear crape on their left arm for thirty days in token of respect for our decd Brother William Clark.
> Resolved that the Lodge be in mourning for ninety days in token of respect of our decd Brother William Clark— the Lodge was closed in due form.

When St. Louis Lodge No. 111 returned its charter to the Mother Grand Lodge of Pennsylvania and applied for a charter from Tennessee, Clark by this act became a member of

Missouri Lodge No. 12, under the Grand Lodge of Tennessee. This was October 3, 1815. The following year General Clark erected on the East side of Main Street (now block 10, between Pine and Olive) a brick house of two stories, the sixth brick building erected in St. Louis, 21 feet front and 32 feet deep; the lower floor was occupied as a counting-house, while the second story was divided into two rooms, access to which was had from below by a staircase in the southeast corner. It was in this building that Missouri Lodge No. 12 met for a period of two years.

Several causes combined to bring about the end of Saint Louis Lodge No. 111. The Mother Grand Lodge was too far distant to feel that kinship necessary to keep up interest; the distance prevented returns being made promptly, and deprived the lodge of representation in the Grand Lodge. It was difficult to transport the annual dues safely. Many of the members were engaged in the War of 1812 against England, and finally, the most prominent member, General Meriwether Lewis, died in 1809.

The names of those who made up Lodge No. 111 are:

Thomas Fiveash Riddick, Senior Warden, first Grand Master of the Grand Lodge of Missouri, Father of the Public School system, and leading citizen.

Rufus Easton, Roman Lodge No. 82 (N. Y.), Charter member of Kaskaskia (Western Star No. 107), First Postmaster in the Territory, and Junior Warden.

Frederick Bates, Governor of Missouri, Secretary of the Territory, Recorder, Secretary of State and the second Master of No. 111.

Alexander McNair, first Governor of Missouri.

John Coons, member of the Territorial Assembly of 1816, and Junior Warden of 111 in 1809.

Joseph V. Garnier, Clerk of the Supreme Court and Secretary of the lodge.

General William Clark, Territorial Governor and Superintendent of Indian affairs, already mentioned.

Silas Bent, Presiding Judge of Common Pleas, County Clerk, and father of Charles Bent, Military Governor of New Mexico.

Risdon H. Price, St. Louis merchant.

Jeremiah Connor, Sheriff of St. Louis and later named in charter as an officer of No. 12.

Dr. Bernard G. Farrar, Judge of the Court of Common Pleas and pioneer physician.

Major Wm. Christy, first Register of Lands.

Judge Wm. C. Carr, Judge of Circuit Court.

Joseph Charless, first editor west of the Mississippi (The Missouri Gazette).

Several of the early French settlers were affiliated with No. 111; some of these received their degrees in this lodge, while others affiliated from sister lodges. Gabriel and Rene Paul, Charles F. Billon, Rene Perdreauville and Pierre Chouteau, Jr., were of the latter class, the first three having received their degrees in Lodge L'Aménité No. 73, in Philadelphia.

The decease of Lodge No. 111 was followed by a period of inactivity. The War of 1812 was soon over and the military forces of the United States, concentrated at points up and down the Mississippi River, were ordered to barracks at the military post in St. Louis. Commerce up and down the Mississippi and Ohio Rivers began to increase and the fur trade brought many new settlers to the Mississippi Valley.

The first mention of the formation of a new lodge at St. Louis is contained in the Proceedings of the Grand Lodge of Tennessee under date of October 3, 1815:

> Ordered, That a Dispensation issue to Brothers Joshua Norvell, Joshua Pilcher and Thomas Brady, to open a Lodge in the Town of St. Louis, in the Missouri Territory, under the name of "Missouri Lodge No. 12."
>
> The Dispensation was signed by Robert Searcy, G. M.;

James Trimble, S. G. W.; David Irwin, J. G. W.; Wilkins Tannehill, Grand Secretary; J. C. MacLemore, Grand Treasurer. On October 8, 1816, the Proceedings note the following action concerning No. 12: "The By-Laws and a transcript of the proceedings of Missouri Lodge No. 12, were presented and approved, and a charter ordered to be issued to said Lodge."

At the Annual Communication of the Grand Lodge of Tennessee on October 4, 1819, No. 12 was represented by Isaac N. Henry, well-known editor of that day. The returns were regularly made that year according to the record, and in 1820, reported 8 initiations, 7 passings, 5 raisings, 1 admission, a total membership on October 1, 1820, of 40.

The membership as thus constituted included the names of most of the members of No. 111, among which were William Clark, Thomas F. Riddick, Alexander McNair, Wm. Christy, Joseph Garnier, Alexander Stuart, Frederick Bates, Judge Robert Wash and many others. By affiliation and otherwise we find the following names added to the rolls: Major Thompson Douglass, Maryland, paymaster, U. S. A.; Captain Risdon H. Price, Eastern Shore, Md., merchant; Judge Nathaniel B. Tucker, Virginia, Judge Circuit Court; Col. Thomas H. Benton, Nashville, Tenn., lawyer; Capt. Peter Ferguson, Norfolk, Va., Judge of Probate; Dr.

Edward S. Gannt, Surgeon, U. S. A.; John Rice Jones, Judge of Supreme Court; Henry S. Geyer, Hagerstown, Md., lawyer; Sergeant Hall, Cincinnati, O., lawyer and editor; Jonathan Guest, Philadelphia, merchant; William H. Hopkins, Philadelphia, merchant; Wm. Renshaw, Sr., Baltimore, merchant; David B. Hoffman, New York, merchant; Abraham Beck, Albany, N. Y., lawyer; Moses Scott, Ireland, Justice of the Peace; George H. C. Melody, Albany, N. Y.; Joseph C. Lavielle, Harrisburg, Pa., architect; Daniel C. Boss, Pittsburg, Pa., merchant; William G. Pettus, Virginia, lawyer.

According to Frederick L. Billon, an accurate historian, the following received degrees in Missouri No. 12:

Edward Bates, Virginia, lawyer; Stephen Rector, surveyor; James Kennerly, Virginia, merchant; James Howard Penrose, Philadelphia; John F. Ryland, Detroit; Amos J. Bruce, Virginia; John D. Daggett, Massachusetts; George Morton, Scotland; Thomas Andrews, Pittsburg; Thornton Grimsley, Kentucky; John Walls; Walter B. Alexander, Virginia; Joseph C. White; William L. Long; William K. Rule, Kentucky; Robert P. Farris, Nattick, Mass.; Isaac A. Letcher, Virginia; William Clarkson, Virginia; James F. Spencer;

William Stark, Kentucky; John E. Tholozan, France; Peter Haldeman, Kentucky; John Jones; David Kneeland; Hart Fellows; Henry Rollins; William LeNeve; Philip Rocheblave; William Hughes; Joseph Walters; George Blanchard; John Hay (?); John Wallace, Phineas James; John J. Douberman; Zenas Smith; Thomas Berry; Moses B. Wall; Joseph M. Yard.

Missouri Lodge No. 12 had been meeting in the house of William Clark, but in 1817, Major Thompson Douglass, a very active Mason and useful citizen, and at the time Master of the lodge, agreed to erect a more commodious hall for the use of the lodge if they would consent to occupy it. An agreement was reached and he erected a two-story brick building on the north side of Elm Street, between Main and Second, which building was occupied by this lodge and its successor (Missouri No. 1) for a period of sixteen years, when, due to the anti-masonic excitement, the lodge was forced to give up its charter. This building was a dwelling house, with four rooms above and four below; above was the attic used as the lodge room. In this room was organized the first Royal Arch Chapter west of the Mississippi River, Missouri Chapter No. 1 (still in existence); here also in 1825, came General

Marquis de Lafayette; and it was in this room the Grand Lodge met and conferred honorary membership upon him and his son.

Little evidence of the activity of this lodge is discoverable by a search of the files of newspapers during the five years of its existence. It did, however, march publicly and attend the funeral of Captain Thomas Ramsey, U. S. A., member of Cincinnati Lodge No. 12, who was killed by Captain Martin in the duel of August 17, 1818. The Feast of St. John the Evangelist was observed, Dec. 27, 1819, at which time the lodge marched in procession from the lodge-room to the "long-room at Bennetts Hotel" where an oration was delivered.

By the year 1821, there were, or had existed in the State of Missouri, the following lodges:

MISSOURI LODGE NO. 12, descendant of St. Louis No. 111, located at St. Louis, Mo., under the Grand Lodge of Tennessee.

SAINT CHARLES NO. 28, located at St. Charles, Mo., and chartered by Grand Lodge of Tennessee.

JOACHIM LODGE NO. 25, located at Herculaneum, Mo., under the Grand Lodge of Tennessee.

UNITY LODGE, later to be given the number "6," located at Jackson, Mo., and under dispensation from the Grand Lodge of Indiana.

HARMONY LODGE, to be made No. 4 on Missouri roster, located at Louisiana, Mo.; petition for dispensation had been made to Tennessee, but was never granted.

POTOSI LODGE No. 39, located at Potosi, Mo., and chartered by the Grand Lodge of Kentucky.

LOUISIANA LODGE No. 109, located at St. Genevieve, Mo., chartered in 1805 by the Grand Lodge of Pennsylvania, inactive, but charter was not arrested until June 7, 1824.

Many new sections of the State were being opened to settlement and this, with the creation of a State Government in 1820, created a demand in the hearts of the members of the fraternity for a Grand Lodge of their own. On Washington's Birthday, 1821, the preliminary convention was held looking towards the organization of the Grand Lodge of Missouri.

In the Reprint of the Minutes of the Grand Lodge of Pennsylvania Vol. II, pp. 353-4; Vol. III, pp. 277-8, we find references to Louisiana Lodge No. 111:

Philadelphia, Thursday 15 Sept. A.D. 1808.
Grand Lodge of Pennsylvania,
Grand Extra Communication.

The R. W. Grand Master informed the Brethren that they had been convened for the purpose of taking into consideration a Petition which had been received praying for a Warrant for holding a lodge at the Town of St. Louis in the Territory of Louisiana. Said Petition was thereupon read, praying for a Warrant for holding a lodge at the town of St. Louis aforesaid, to be named and styled "Saint Louis Lodge," and that His Excellency Meriwether Lewis, Esqr. Governor of the said Territory of Louisiana, might be named Master; Bror. Thomas Fiveash Riddick, Senior Warden, and Bror. Rufus Easton, Junior Warden of the same.

Which Petition being in due form and recommended by the Louisiana Lodge No. 109, agreeable to the regulations of this Grand Lodge, it was on Motion made and seconded, Resolved, That the prayer of the Petitioners be granted, and that Bror. Grand Secretary make out a Warrant accordingly, and that the said lodge be No. 111.

Philadelphia, 6th Sept. 1813.

The Grand Secretary Reported, That agreeably to the 22d Article of the Regulations of this Grand Lodge, he had on the 7th ultimo, notified the undermentioned Lodge of their Delinquency by a circular Communication to them as follows, to wit: Article 22d of the Regulations of the Grand Lodge of Pennsylvania. Any Lodge in arrears with this Grand Lodge of two years dues, shall be notified thereof by the Grand Secretary, and if their dues are not discharged within Six Months from the Date of such notice, the warrant of such Lodge shall be considered as suspended, and unless satisfactory reasons for such neglect are adducted to the Grand Lodge at the next Quarterly Communication, the Warrant of such lodge shall be Vacated.

109 St. Genevieve, Louisiana Territory.
111 Town of St. Louis, Louisiana Territory.

Philadelphia, 7 August 1813.

WORSHIPFUL SIR AND BROTHER,

Agreeably to the 22d Article of the Regulations of the Grand Lodge, "whereof the foregoing is a copy" you are hereby notified, that your lodge is in arrears with the Grand Lodge for more than two years dues, and that if the same are not paid within six months from Date hereof, the Warrant of your lodge will be considered as suspended, and unless satisfactory reasons for such neglect shall be adduced to the Grand Lodge at their Quarterly Communication in March next, your Warrant will be then Vacated.

I am &c

(Signed) GEORGE A. BAKER,
Grand Secretary.

On April 4th, 1814, the following action was had:

On motion made and seconded,

Resolved, That further time be granted to the following Delinquent Lodges for completing their Returns and paying up their Grand Lodge dues, Viz:
Lodge No. 111, Town of St. Louis, Louisiana Territory.

So far as we are able to learn, the members of No. 111 are yet indebted to the Grand Lodge of Pennsylvania, unless death and the statute of limitations may be considered as a bar to the collection!

CHAPTER X

MISSOURI'S MASONIC NEIGHBORS

IT MUST not be supposed that while Missouri was showing such remarkable signs of Masonic activity, our brothers in neighboring states and territories were at all behind. The influence of the surrounding States of Indiana, Tennessee and Kentucky, particularly Tennessee, was of extreme importance. Masonic membership was largely composed of men of southern extraction, who looked largely to their mother states for Masonic standards. The majority of those forming the first Grand Lodge received their degrees in lodges under Tennessee charter; how natural that the laws, customs, and traditions of this Grand Lodge should be copied, imitated and utilized by Missourians.

Yet, certain happenings lead us to believe that brethren, schooled by standards received through other Grand Lodges, possessed influence sufficient to sway, and even to change, some of the fundamentals expressed by the Grand Lodge of Tennessee.

It is necessary, while studying our own conditions, to see what transpired in the great territory which surrounded us; in this, we do not propose to go into a mass of detail, but merely to call to attention the existence of certain other Grand Lodges, taking occasion to refer to the long list of distinguished men who occupied places of honor in the official councils of the fraternity.

The leading men were active in the organization of the first Grand Lodges; the list is of honorable names, and one of which the fraternity may always be proud. It includes the names of General Lewis Cass, Israel Putnam, Col. Joseph Hamilton Daviess, Henry Clay, Robert Livingston, General Andrew Jackson, Governor Shadrach Bond, and many others, equally as important although hardly so prominent in the public eye. What these men did for Freemasonry in early days can never be measured, nor can we of a later day pay homage to them according to their merit. Their gift to the Craft was that of sacrifice, always freely and voluntarily made without the hope of fee or reward, except it be that reward of satisfaction derived from accomplishment.

Kentucky

THE Grand Lodge of Kentucky was the child of the Grand Lodge of Virginia, the latter jurisdiction having chartered five lodges in the State of Kentucky prior to the formation of a Grand Lodge by Kentucky. Masonry first entered Kentucky when a charter was given to Lexington Lodge No. 25, at Lexington, Kentucky, November 17, 1788. A preliminary meeting for the purpose of organization was held in Lexington, September 8, 1800, and a little more than a month later, October 16, 1800, the first communication of the Grand Lodge of Kentucky was held, presided over by M. W. Bro. James Morrison, "the oldest Past Master present" and the second Grand Master of that State.

Colonel James Morrison was a soldier of the Revolution, a gentleman of the old school, liberal, a money-maker, close friend of Andrew Jackson, and founder of the Kentucky Bible Society, which in 1817 became the American Bible Society. At his death he left $40,000 to erect a building at Transylvania University, and $20,000 to endow a professorship.

The Grand Lodge selected as their first Grand Master William Murray, eminent lawyer, Attorney General of the State and one who prosecuted the inquiry into the conspiracy of Aaron Burr; two Master Masons who later became Grand Masters of this Grand Lodge, Henry Clay and John Allen, defended Burr.

A most interesting figure in Kentucky Masonry was Colonel Joseph Hamilton Daviess, elected Grand Master at the Annual Communication held in 1811; the newly installed Grand Master delivered an appropriate address and charge, the last words ever spoken before the Grand Lodge over which he presided, for the hand of fortune destined him to give up his life in defence of his country at the Battle of Tippecanoe.

Daviess was a Virginian, born March 4, 1774, coming to Kentucky with his family in 1779; he had a splendid education, was versed in the art of oratory and had a wonderful future. He had married Anne Marshall, sister of Chief Justice John Marshall, in 1803, and after 1809 made his home at Lexington, Kentucky. In 1792, he became a mounted volunteer, his duties being to guard transportation of provisions to forts located north of the Ohio River. It was on one of these missions that he had his first fight with the Indians, when with reckless courage he recaptured his horse while under a shower of bullets.

It was he who prosecuted Burr at Frankfort, Kentucky, for treasonable conspiracy, opposing Henry Clay, in what was termed a "splendid intellectual combat."

Ohio

THE Grand Lodge of Ohio came into existence as the result of a preliminary convention held at Chillicothe, Ohio, January 4, 1808, at which six lodges were represented; one lodge in that State, American Union, was not represented and did not join the Grand Lodge of Ohio for many years. January 7, 1808, Grand Officers were elected, M. W. Bro. Rufus Putnam becoming Grand Master.

Louisiana

MAY 15, 1812, Lodge La Parfaite Union, No. 29, issued a circular to the several lodges throughout the Territory of Louisiana, inviting the several lodges then existing to assemble and deliberate on the necessity and wisdom of establishing a Grand Lodge for Louisiana. At the assembly held June 13, 1812, five lodges were represented; La Parfaite Union No. 29 (South Carolina); La Charité No. 93; La Concorde No. 117; La Perseverance No. 118 and L'Etoile Polaire No. 129, all of the latter lodges having been chartered by the Grand Lodge of Pennsylvania. This Grand Lodge was embryonic and lasted only a few years; the first Grand Master was Peter Francis DuBourg.

Peter Francis DuBourg was a brother of the "Most Reverend Archbishop Louis William V. DuBourg," the latter the first Archbishop of the Roman Catholic Church to be assigned to St. Louis Territory. M. W. Bro. Peter F. DuBourg seems to have made a very satisfactory Grand Master. He was born at Cape Francois, on the Island of San Domingo, where a large number of Louisiana Masons received their degrees, having been compelled by the Revolution to flee the country.

Freemasonry in Louisiana has had a very checkered career from the time its first lodges were organized; conflicting jurisdictions, racial inequalities and sympathies, religious barriers and intolerance, and the inter-meddling of clandestine and some recognized rites of Freemasonry, all united to make the path rough, the going hard. It has only been in recent years that Masonry has begun to assume its proper position in this State.

Tennessee

THE only Grand Lodge in the United States, according to our information, organized with the full authority and approval of the

Mother Grand Lodge, was the Grand Lodge of Tennessee.

A convention was held December 27, 1813, attended by the representatives of eight lodges, which had previously been working under charters from the Grand Lodge of North Carolina; these lodges were: Tennessee Lodge No. 2; Greenville No. 3; Newport No. 4; Overton No. 5; King Solomon No. 6; Hiram No. 7; Cumberland No. 8; Western Star No. 9. The convention having assembled at Knoxville on the above date, a Charter or Deed of Relinquishment, issued by the authority of the Grand Lodge of North Carolina, was read September 30, 1813, ceding all authority and jurisdiction over that Territory, and giving assent to the formation of the Grand Lodge of Tennessee. Thomas Claiborne became the first Grand Master.

The most distinguished of all Tennessee Masons was the hero of New Orleans, General Andrew Jackson, who later became Grand Master of the Grand Lodge of Tennessee. He was the son of a widow, left with three sons to support following the Revolution; two of these sons later fell in battle. After the fall of Charleston and the defeat of Colonel Buford of Virginia, permission was given to five American women to carry provisions and administer relief to prisoners on a prison ship; Andrew Jackson's mother was one of the volunteers, braving a pestilence, which later planted in her system a disease of prison fever, from the effects of which she later died, a martyr to humanity and patriotism. Her only son was left to the mercies of charity, yet he was later to be President of the United States, while his mother was to sleep in an unmarked grave.

It was General Jackson, who in 1825 during the visit of General Lafayette to the Mississippi Valley, had the pleasure of introducing the great Frenchman to the members of his own Grand Lodge. Jackson once had serious difficulty with our own Brother Thomas H. Benton, but happily before their death all animosity ceased and they became the greatest of friends.

Indiana

THE honor of bringing Masonry to Indiana belongs to General W. Johnson, a distinguished member of old Abraham Lodge at Louisville, Kentucky. The first Indiana Lodge was organized at Vincennes, August 27, 1807. In 1816, Indiana Territory became a state and the following year, December 3, 1817, the nine Indiana lodges met at Corydon, Indiana, for the purpose of organizing a Grand Lodge for that

State. On January 12, 1818, representatives from these lodges again met and formed a Grand Lodge, electing as Grand Master, Alexander Buckner, better known to Missourians as responsible for the institution of Unity Lodge No. 6, at Jackson, Missouri.

Masonry in Indiana, during the period under discussion, claimed many of the best citizens of the Territory; they were to be found in all walks of life, and the record of their activities is a credit to the Masonic fraternity of Indiana. The names of Colonel Joseph Bartholomew, General W. Johnson, Henry Vanderburgh and other leading citizens and Freemasons are indelibly linked with the history of the Hoosier State.

Ohio & Lewis Cass

"I, Lewis Cass, beg to be admitted to the sacred mysteries of Freemasonry, if found Worthy.
Marietta, Nov. 7, 1803.   Lewis Cass"

THIS was the petition for Masonic degrees, signed by General Lewis Cass, which later caused him to be initiated in American Union Lodge No. 1, at Marietta, Ohio, December 5, 1803, and resulting later in his being made Grand Master of Ohio, January 10, 1810, a position he held until his removal to Michigan in 1813. In 1826, at the time of the organization of a Grand Lodge in the latter State, he became the first Grand Master.

General Cass was born in New Hampshire in 1782, son of Captain Jonathan Cass of the Revolution. In 1800 he came to Marietta, Ohio, where he studied law under the supervision of Governor Meigs, being admitted to the bar at the age of twenty. He began the practice of law at Zanesville, and soon acquired a splendid practice and a wide reputation; his election to the Legislature in 1806 started his political career.

He was a member of the committee charged to inquire into the supposed treasonable activities of Aaron Burr, and the report which he drew up and presented to President Thomas Jefferson was probably responsible for his being named United States Marshal of that State in 1807. He was a soldier in the War of 1812, starting as a Colonel and ending his career as a Brigadier-General. At the close of the war he was stationed at Detroit, becoming Governor of the Territory in 1813; he made a splendid Governor for the Territory, his administration being distinguished by twenty-two Indian treaties, cession to the United States of the immense regions of the Northwest, new surveys, new roads, military posts established, erection of light-houses, the organization of townships and counties, and many other accomplishments calculated to induce prosperity in the Territory.

President Andrew Jackson, in 1831, appointed him Secretary of War, and as such, it fell to him to suppress the Black Hawk insurrection. In 1836, he became Minister to France; he resigned this position after six years' service, and in 1845 was elected to the United States Senate. He became the Democratic candidate for President in 1848, but was defeated. In the Senate he was a strong ally of Henry Clay; he was re-elected to the Senate and in 1852 was again a candidate for the Presidency. In 1857 he was made Secretary of State under President Buchanan, but through the failure of the President to reinforce and provision Fort Sumter, he resigned, terminating a public career of fifty-six years. He died June 11, 1866, at the age of eighty-four, and was buried by the fraternity with Masonic honors.

Illinois

WHILE organized Masonry came to Illinois before it did to Missouri, it was Missouri which organized the first Grand Lodge. The Grand Lodge of Missouri, organized in

1821, was followed by a Grand Lodge of Illinois in 1824, a Grand Lodge of very short life which eventually went down with the antimasonic storm which raged during the thirties. A majority of those lodges, members of this first Grand Lodge of Illinois, had been chartered by the Grand Lodge of Missouri, which necessitated their being taken under Missouri's wing, following the failure of the first Illinois Grand Lodge.

The outstanding character in Illinois Masonry of this period was Governor Shadrach Bond, the first Grand Master of Freemasons, and the first Governor of Illinois. Bond was a noble, talented pioneer, capable, honest and God-fearing. He was born in Frederick County, Maryland, in 1773, coming to Illinois in 1794, where he resided with his uncle, Shadrach Bond, Sr. He was a large portly man of more than two hundred pounds, standing six feet high, commanding in appearance, dignified in action, with dark complexion and jet-black hair.

In his early life, he was elected a member of the Territorial General Assembly, which met at Vincennes; in 1812, he was the first delegate from the Illinois Territory to Congress, where his exertions secured the passage of an act authorizing citizens of the Territory to rights of pre-emption, an act which greatly encouraged immigration. Bond next became Receiver of Public Moneys at Kaskaskia and, when Illinois was granted statehood, became its first Governor.

As Governor, he was first to suggest the propriety of connecting Lake Michigan and the Mississippi River. He died April 11, 1830, mourned by the citizens and Masons of the State of Illinois.

Our own Past Grand Master George H. C. Melody officiated at the first installation of officers of the first Grand Lodge of Illinois. Missouri's dealings with her neighbor on the east have always been friendly and harmonious.

CHAPTER XI
MASONRY CROSSES THE MISSOURI

THE logical situation for a future metropolis of Missouri was that Territory which lies east of the present site of the City of St. Charles, Missouri; bounded on one side by the Mississippi River and on the other by the Missouri, the site furnished an outlet to any section of the new Territory by water. But fortune, that sullen and unexplainable mistress of human destiny, entered in, and St. Charles is to-day the St. Charles of 1821, somewhat overgrown. The demands of commerce have forced railroads upon her thoroughfares, transportation demanded the building of a bridge spanning the Missouri, but sufficient of the olden days is left to give the visitor a conception of the village when it was the capital of Missouri, when prosperity hovered over the city as a cloud, bringing the dream of the wonderful city that was to arise.

Into this city of dreams, nestled under a hill, came scattered members of the Masonic fraternity, preparing the way for a society which knew no race, no creed, no politics, no religion, a doctrine badly needed at such a time, when French, Spanish, Americans, negroes and others were endeavoring to understand each other and live together in harmony and in peace.

By 1818, sufficient members of this fraternity had reached St. Charles as to warrant the proposed organization of a lodge; had not St. Louis, the rival city on the south, a lodge? And was not St. Genevieve the home of a lodge? And even scraggly Herculaneum had dared to make request of the Grand Lodge of Tennessee for a dispensation! Why not St. Charles, which destiny had marked as queen of all the cities of the West?

Only scattered records of this first lodge in St. Charles exist, for time and fire, ignorance and carelessness, are the enemies of history. This is unfortunate, for this lodge had the honor of being the first chartered north of the Missouri River, and one of the three Tennessee lodges which assisted in organizing the Grand Lodge of Missouri.

So far as written records go, Freemasonry in St. Charles dates from July 5, 1819, at which time according to the Grand Lodge of Tennessee, there was "received a petition from sundry brethren, Master Masons, residing at St.

Charles, Missouri Territory, praying for a Dispensation to form a new lodge at that place, to be called, 'St. Charles Lodge No. 28,' which being read, it was ordered that the prayer of the petitioners be granted."

Three months later, October 5, 1819, the dispensation and records of St. Charles Lodge No. 28 were returned to the Mother Grand Lodge for inspection, with a petition praying for a perpetual charter. Their returns were approved, although nothing is said as to the nature of the work done. A charter was granted and No. 28 became a regular lodge.

In 1820, No. 28 failed to make return, no reason for which was given, but appended to the report of the Grand Lodge of Tennessee in 1822 is the statement:

> Returns; St. Charles No. 28—initiated 12; passed 10; raised 11; admitted 3; total number of members 27. Returns from September 1819, to March 1821, when said Lodge joined the Grand Lodge of Missouri.

Of the membership of No. 28, at the time the charter was issued, we can only be positive of those named in the charter:

>   BENJAMIN EMMONS, *Master*
>   BENNETT PALMER, *Senior Warden*
>   JOHN PAYNE, *Junior Warden*

From other papers, discovered in the effects of the lodge, we find the names of other members previous to their joining the Grand Lodge of Missouri; whether they came into the lodge as initiates or affiliates is left to our imagination and further research. Among these names are:

    Joseph Evans   Will G. Shade
    Henry Hayes   Nathaniel Simonds
    Benjamin Owen   John Stoddard
    J. H. Penrose   Samuel Taylor
    William G. Pettus   Rowland Willard
    N. Riddick   Andrew Wilson
    Joseph W. Garraty

and probably N. Rice, Daniel Howland, Abraham S. Platt *and* Benjamin Walker.

Even these figures account for but 20 of the 27 known members of the lodge as reported up to and including March 1821; it is probable that Horace Barber, William Smith, G. W. Ash, and Samuel Keithley, who had received some degrees in the early part of 1821, were included in the list of 27 members; if so, this would leave but 3 unaccounted for.

On receipt of an invitation, extended by Missouri Lodge No. 1 of St. Louis, to attend and participate in a preliminary convention, looking to the organization of a Grand Lodge of Missouri, St. Charles Lodge No. 28 appointed representatives. The official proceedings do not give the names of the delegates, except to mention Brother Nathaniel Simonds of No. 28, named as one of a committee to draft a Constitution. At the meeting held April 24 following, Brother Abm. S. Platt is mentioned as representing No. 28; William G. Pettus acted as Grand Treasurer, *pro tem*, but is not noted as representing No. 28. . The original Committee from No. 28 must have consisted of Simonds, Pettus, and Platt. Pettus proved very active in the first few years of the Grand Lodge, as shown by the Proceedings.

Then came events which almost destroyed the harmony of the Grand Lodge and which make it appear that the Grand Lodge was the creature of Missouri Lodge No. 1, and organized by *two* lodges of the jurisdiction! There is no question but that Missouri Lodge No. 1 dominated the Grand Lodge of Missouri during its early period, and that it continued to dominate it just as long as it was possible to do so, leaving the rural lodges to bear the brunt of the fight in the anti-masonic warfare, during the Morgan excitement. It was ever thus; those who seek honors are first to desert in hour of trouble.

The Grand Lodge of Missouri met, organized, and seemingly every one was happy (unless the Grand Lodge of Tennessee was an exception). Brother Thompson Douglass, in order to legalize the lodges, now under Missouri charter, introduced the following resolution:

Resolved, That the M. W. G. Master be authorized on the receipt of any Charter or Warrant of Dispensation from any Lodge under this jurisdiction, to grant them a new charter or dispensation, under their private seals, attested by the Grand Secretary, which shall be their authority for such Lodge to continue their labors, until the next regular Communication of the Grand Lodge, but no longer unless the Grand Lodge shall then confirm the same.

Then St. Charles Lodge, no doubt stirred by the fact that at the organization of the Grand Lodge, *all but one of the stations were filled by St. Louis members*, prepared and submitted the following petition:

To Thomas F. Riddick, Most Worshipful Grand Master of the Grand Lodge of the State of Missouri:—

The undersigned members of the late St. Charles Lodge No. 28, having surrendered their charters to the Grand Lodge of Tennessee, and conceiving that they cannot work under those circumstances as a regular Lodge without the permission of the Grand Lodge of this State. They are desirous of continuing a Lodge in the town of St. Charles to be named Hiram.

That in consequence of this desire they pray for letters of dispensation or a warrant of constitution, to empower

them to assemble, as a legal Lodge, to discharge the duties of Masonry in a regular and constitutional manner according to the original forms of the order, and the regulations of the Grand Lodge. That they have nominated and do recommend William G. Pettus, to be first Master, Joseph Evans to be first Senior Warden, and Rowland Willard to be first Junior Warden of the said Lodge.
St. Charles, 11th August, 1821.

A warrant of constitution, seemingly such as was authorized under the Douglass resolution, was issued on August 17, 1821, but before it had been delivered to the St. Charles brethren, the lodge held a called meeting on August 19, and adopted the following resolution:

That the order made on the 3rd day of May A.L. 5821, directing the return of the charter to the Grand Lodge of Tennessee, be rescinded, and the Master or other brother officiating as Master, transmit it to the Grand Lodge of the State for the purpose of obtaining letters of dispensation, or a charter from that Grand Lodge.

This is evidently the resolution and petition referred to in the Missouri proceedings of October 1, 1821, but adding the further information;

That St. Charles Lodge having surrendered her charter, was entitled to another one—that the M. W. G. M. had during the recess of the Grand Lodge, granted them a Letter of Dispensation, under which they had declined working, and pray that a Charter of Constitution may be granted them.

The petition was laid over until the following day, when Brother Archibald Gamble smoothed the difficulty over by two resolutions, one authorizing the Grand Master to issue a charter to the new No. 3 and the other authorizing them to attend the present Grand Annual Communication, recognizing their membership in the Grand Lodge by a preliminary clause in the resolution, beginning: "That as the St. Charles Lodge No. 28, was one of the convention forming this Grand Lodge, etc." Gamble, in rendering this service, was doing only what he was required to do, he being the legal proxy of William G. Pettus, the Master of No. 3.

At this October 6, 1821, session to smooth out the difficulties encountered during the preceding months, Benjamin Emmons of No. 3 was elected Grand Senior Warden and promptly declined.

It was not until October 11, 1822, over a year following the organization of the Grand Lodge, that a satisfactory charter was issued to Hiram No. 3 and the controversy was closed, so far as the records show.

The strength of Hiram No. 3 was not in the class with the strength of the Illustrious Tyrian whose strength was the support of King Solomon, for Hiram No. 3 existed only until April 4, 1826. After the anti-masonic episode, a new charter was sought, granted, and St. Charles took up the work under the old name of "Hiram Lodge," but with the number "23." October 16, 1846, the second Hiram ceased to exist. A *third* Hiram appeared May 10, 1850, and departed May 1862. "Hiram" had but three lives to give, and when the lodge was later resurrected, it became Palestine No. 241, under which name the St. Charles brethren continue to carry on the work of Freemasonry begun over a century ago.

CHAPTER XII

PRE-GRAND-LODGE LODGES

FOUR Missouri lodges deserve mention, not for what they accomplished, but for their pioneering efforts, seemingly necessary whenever Freemasonry obtains a foot-hold in new territory. Not one of the four (instituted by outside Grand Lodges) maintained its existence under the original name; in most cases, other lodges took up the work where these lodges failed.

During the period preceding statehood, the village of Potosi was almost as well known as any of the towns in Missouri. Just across a creek from old Mine-a-Breton, it became the county seat of Washington County. It received its name from Moses Austin, a celebrated pioneer of that territory. It is said to have had an appearance possessed by none of its rivals of the time, the town containing many splendid buildings, especially "a Court-house built on the Doric Order, costing $7,000." Potosi had wonderful dreams of a future and even went so far as to aspire to be the capital city of the State; three stores, two distilleries, a steam flour mill, nine lead furnaces, a saw mill and a post-office were listed as the principal town assets. Brothers Stephen Austin, John Rice Jones, Aaron Elliott and John W. Honey were residents of Potosi during parts of their lives.

In August, 1816, Andrew Scott and others petitioned for a lodge at Potosi; the petition was made out and sent to the Grand Lodge of Kentucky, the only other lodge in existence in Missouri at the time being Louisiana Lodge at St. Genevieve, which at the time was inactive. The charter was granted, Scott being named as first Master; Potosi Lodge appears on the roll of Kentucky lodges as late as 1818, but was subsequently dropped; the charter being returned to the Grand Lodge of Kentucky in 1819.

Brother Scott was Clerk of the House in the fourth and last Territorial Assembly. He was one of the trustees of Potosi Academy, incorporated in 1817. About this time Scott accepted a position in the Territory of Arkansas. Interest in the work waned, and Potosi Lodge was added to the long list of dead lodges, whose fall has been due to their being chartered by Grand Masters who failed to investigate their possibilities for future success.

The *ancient* Herculaneum was situated along the Mediterranean, the *later* Herculaneum along the Mississippi River; as volcanic lava covered the ancient city, so did Masonic lethargy cover the lead-mining village of Herculaneum. In 1819, three shot mining towers were in successful operation on the perpendicular bluff which overhung the town; the steep precipice was on the bank of the Mississippi River and did not necessitate the erection of the usual shot-tower.

In 1819 an application was made to the Grand Lodge of Tennessee for a charter for a lodge to be located at Herculaneum; the Grand Lodge of Tennessee, always free with its charters, granted the request on October 6, 1819, and named the following officers:

>Wm. F. Roberts, *Master*
>Seth Converse, *Senior Warden*
>Wm. Bates, *Junior Warden*

Joachim Lodge was No. 25 on the Tennessee Register; the name was taken from a small stream which flowed near the village. The lodge can really claim to date from January 4, 1819, at which time a dispensation was issued "to sundry brethren residing at Herculaneum, Missouri Territory."

Returns of 1820, made to the Grand Lodge

of Tennessee, show that Joachim Lodge initiated 3; passed 2; raised 2; admitted 1; and numbered seventeen members during that year (Oct. 1820). In July 1821, Joachim Lodge wrote the Grand Lodge of Tennessee asking to be absolved from all relations with it, as they had become members of the new Grand Lodge of Missouri. The Mother Grand Lodge said "which request is, in the opinion of your committee, *unreasonable*, and ought not be granted."

The only names of known members of this lodge which are on record, are those of William Bates, William F. Roberts, James S. Beaumont, Henry Cellinger and Seth Converse. The charter of the lodge was arrested by the Grand Lodge of Missouri in 1825, it being at that time No. 2 on the Missouri Register.

Wm. Bates represented the lodge at the preliminary convention in February 1821; he was again present at the April meeting, at which time he was made Junior Grand Warden, returning, May 4, 1821, for installation.

In October 1821, we find from the records of the Grand Lodge "The M. W. G. M. presented a communication from Joachim Lodge No. 2, and also from Brother William F. Roberts, Senior Warden of said lodge, received by him in vacation, relative to a difficulty between some of the members of that lodge, which was read and laid on the table." William Bates appeared at the meeting on the following day, and the second day following, announced "that all differences between the members of said lodge, the subjects presented to the Grand Lodge, had since been reconciled."

Bates appeared again as Grand Junior Warden at the meeting April 1822; it is evident from the monies received by the Grand Secretary from Joachim Lodge in 1822, that the lodge had but 15 members in 1822. Brother Melody visited the lodge for the purpose of giving it instruction during this year. In October 1823, the Grand Lodge, displeased at the negligence of No. 25 in not submitting reports, adopted a resolution that unless reports were received before the next semi-annual communication they would be "stricken from the books of the Grand Lodge," a procedure which was postponed until October 1824, and again until April 1825 when it was finally "stricken."

The death of William Bates, leading spirit of No. 25, during the year 1822, was no doubt the cause of the early departure of No. 25. The Grand Lodge brought the news of his death to the attention of the members and requested them to go into mourning for the usual ninety days. The lodge itself must have gone into perpetual mourning for we know of no further action taken by it!

A lodge the early history of which has been somewhat shrouded in a misty haze of ignorance is Harmony Lodge No. 4, located at Louisiana, Missouri. This lodge should have been, by right, one of those which organized the Grand Lodge of Missouri; in fact, there was some feeling evident in the matter, if correspondence at the time is to be taken as evidence.

According to the original records of this lodge, its formation was first broached "at a meeting held at the storehouse of William Alley, in the town of Louisiana, for the purpose of taking into consideration the expediency or inexpediency of adopting means to establish a lodge of Free and Accepted Masons at this place."

These records show that there were present on this occasion "James C. Phelan, John R. Carter, Albion T. Crow, Ezra Hunt, Lawrence A. January, William Alley, Richard Bruer, and Michael J. Noyes, Masters in Masonry."

The following proceedings were then had:

> Ordered that Michael J. Noyes be appointed Moderator and Richard Bruer Secretary to this meeting.
>
> Resolved unanimously that proper measures be taken to organize and establish a lodge of Free and Accepted Masons at this place.

Resolved, unanimously, that a petition be forwarded to the Grand Lodge of Tennessee, for the purpose of obtaining letters of Dispensation, and that the expense thereof be defrayed jointly by the members of this meeting.

Resolved, unanimously, that Brother Ezra Hunt be recommended as Master, Brother Michael J. Noyes as Senior Warden, and Brother Albion T. Crow as Junior Warden.

Resolved, that Brothers James C. Phelan, John R. Carter, and Ezra Hunt be appointed a Committee to draft a petition to be forwarded the Grand Lodge of Tennessee in order to procure letters of Dispensation.

The Committee appointed to draft a petition, attended to the duties of their appointment and reported a petition which was unanimously adopted.

Meeting dissolved this 8th day of January, A.L. 5821.

MICHAEL J. NOYES, *Moderator.*

Attest:

RICHARD BRUER, *Sec'y.*

On this same date, the committee, instead of drawing up the one petition addressed to the Grand Lodge of Tennessee, drew up an additional petition, the second one addressed to the Grand Lodge of Missouri—*not yet in existence.* It is evident from this that news had gotten about concerning the proposed meeting on February 22 to consider the question of a Grand Lodge for Missouri.

The members must have been somewhat wroth at their failure to be admitted among the elect. On the occasion of the Grand Lodge organization, the proposed Master, Ezra Hunt, wrote the Grand Secretary, under date of October 4, 1821, asking whether record had been made of the granting of a charter to Harmony No. 4, which he believed should be done "to prevent any further unpleasant feeling."

The Grand Lodge of Missouri was right in being unwilling to admit the proposed Harmony Lodge until such a time as it had acquired a Masonic entity; it was not (and Worshipful Brother Ezra Hunt, a leading lawyer of that section should have advised the proposed members) a Masonic body. These men were merely an *organization* of Freemasons asking for a dispensation or charter, and until the Grand Lodge of Missouri came into being, it could offer them no consolation.

The charter granted to Harmony Lodge was the first granted to any lodge, except those members of the preliminary convention; it is signed by Thomas F. Riddick, the Grand Master, under date of June 26, 1821. This lodge lasted for a few years and then gave up its charter, but was later rechartered as Perseverance Lodge No. 15; time has proved that the latter name was not well chosen.

The first lawyer to settle in the town of Louisiana was Worshipful Brother Ezra Hunt, who was present on more than one occasion as the representative of his lodge in the Grand Lodge; he was born in Massachusetts in 1790, in the town of Milford, graduating in 1816 at Harvard University. He came West, teaching school in Tennessee for one year, then coming on to St. Louis where he read law in the office of Wm. C. Carr. He went to Pike County in 1819 and was the first lawyer to be admitted to the bar there. He died in 1860, having attended every session of the circuit court from the time of his admission; he was said to have been an honest lawyer, which the historian says "must have been the reason he died a comparatively poor man."

Michael Noyes is listed as a settler in Pike County as early as 1808, coming with a party of South Carolinians.

In 1814, a large settlement having grown up at Jackson, Missouri, it was soon thereafter made the county seat. It was described as "a considerable village on a hill," it "contained between sixty and seventy dwellings, five stores, two shoemaker shops, one tannery, two good schools, one for males and one for females" and "in and around Jackson were more moral, intelligent and truly religious people, than any village or settlement in the territory."

Edmund Rutter and Joseph Frizzell, members of the lodge, established themselves in business in Jackson between the years 1815-20; Samuel Cupple, first Treasurer of Unity Lodge No. 6, purchased from a Mr. Eckhardt, the first store established in the village.

Organized Masonry opened here in 1818, with the arrival of Alexander Buckner; tradition was, that he had left his native state of Indiana as the result of a duel. Before his departure, he had been elected Grand Master (the first) of Indiana. Having removed from the State, his successor was elected in September. Shortly after his arrival in Missouri, he made the acquaintance of George Bullitt, a resident of Jackson, and member of Lodge No. 109 at St. Genevieve; other members of No. 109 lived at Jackson, and, the affairs of the latter lodge being at low ebb, Buckner offered his assistance in securing a dispensation from his own Grand Lodge. Bullitt received his degrees in the lodge at Kaskaskia (No. 107).

The application for dispensation was prepared and signed by the following Master Masons; Alexander Buckner, Edward S. Gannt, Joseph McFerron, Thomas Neale, Samuel Cupples, Joseph F. Gray, George Bullitt, Edmund Rutter, Charles Mulligan, John Cross and John G. Vance. Grand Master John Tipton, in accordance with the request, issued a dispensation under date of December

21, 1820, naming Buckner as Master, Gannt as Senior Warden and McFerron as Junior Warden of a lodge to be held "in the town of Jackson, in Missouri, by the name of Unity Lodge, and authorized Brother Henry Dodge to install the officers of said lodge."

Brother Minor Whitney, who attended the Grand Lodge of Indiana in 1821, must have informed his brethren of the Grand Lodge of the organization of a Grand Lodge of Missouri; the Committee charged with the examination of the records of this lodge U. D. offered a resolution as follows:

> Resolved, That as this Grand Lodge has a perfect confidence in the skill and ability of the brethren of Unity Lodge under dispensation, that they be permitted to separate from this Grand Lodge, and that this Grand Lodge recommend them to the Most Worshipful Grand Lodge of Missouri, to be a chartered lodge.

Two days following the preliminary convention held in St. Louis, February 22, 1821, for the purpose of organizing a Grand Lodge of Missouri, the new lodge was instituted at Jackson by General Henry Dodge of Louisiana Lodge No. 109.

The records of Unity Lodge show that while under dispensation from the Grand Lodge of Indiana, the following degrees were conferred:

PRE-GRAND-LODGE LODGES

BATES, ROBERT; initiated March 10, 1821; passed April 25, 1821; raised June 22, 1821.

CRIDDLE, EDWARD; initiated May 12, 1821; passed April 7, 1821; raised April 16, 1821.

HAYS, JOHN; initiated March 10, 1821; passed April 25, 1821; raised August 18, 1821.

FRIZZELL, JOSEPH; initiated May 12, 1821; passed May 15, 1821; raised May 18, 1821.

JONES, THEODORE; initiated June 7, 1821; passed June 13, 1821; raised June 30, 1821.

NEALE, WILLIAM; initiated August 11, 1821.

RUSSELL, JAMES; initiated March 10, 1821; passed April 17, 1821; raised April 21, 1821.

SEAVERS, CHARLES; initiated July 7, 1821; passed August 25, 1821.

WATKINS, NATHANIEL W.; initiated April 7, 1821; passed April 17, 1821; raised April 27, 1821.

WHITNEY, MINOR M.; initiated April 7, 1821; passed April 17, 1821; raised April 21, 1821.

RANNEY, JOHNSON; admitted from Philatrophic Lodge of Massachusetts, May 12, 1821.

At the Annual Communication of the Grand Lodge of Missouri, held in October, 1821, on motion of Brother Thompson Douglass, it was ordered that a charter be granted to the members of Unity Lodge, and that they be given the Number "six" on the Missouri Register; they continued to work under a "charter of constitution" which was no doubt a dispensation, until April 1822 when they were formally chartered.

CHAPTER XIII

FREEMASONS AND THE STATE CONSTITUTION

FROM the time the Louisiana Purchase was ceded to the United States, the people began to clamor for statehood; the very act of Cession itself set forth statehood as the ultimate goal. That Missouri failed to receive statehood was largely due to certain issues, then in the public mind, which arose to cloud and befog the issue. The great bugaboo of the time was slavery; even then Missouri barely entered the galaxy of stars by a narrow margin, and this, the result of the Missouri Compromise.

The population of Missouri Territory in 1820 was 60,000. Congress passed an act authorizing the inhabitants of the Territory "to take the proper steps to form a Constitution and State Government." The act was passed and approved by the President, Brother James Monroe, March 6, 1820. Under a provision of the act, the question of the election of delegates to the State Convention was left to the people of the Territory, who were to assemble on the first Monday, Tuesday and Wednesday in May, 1820, and select them *viva voce*.

On Monday, June 12, 1820, the delegates thus selected assembled in St. Louis for the purpose of carrying out the Act of Congress. The sessions were held in the long dining room of the Mansion House, leading hotel of the city of St. Louis, located at the corner of Vine and Third Streets, conducted by the popular William Bennett, one time member of Western Star Lodge No. 107, at Kaskaskia. He demitted to Missouri Lodge No. 12, in 1819, when he came to St. Louis to conduct the Mansion House Hotel, a building erected originally in 1816, by Brother and General William Rector, U. S. Surveyor General for his office and residence, but which was remodeled for hotel purposes. This famous hostelry was the scene of many historic events; it was the only ball room afforded the people of St. Louis at the time and here came the leading men of the territory on political or business mission.

The Masonic membership of several members of this Convention has not been entirely cleared up, but of the names listed below, we have the official written records:

County of St. Louis: Pierre Chouteau, Jr., Bernard Pratte, Jr., Thomas F. Riddick, William Rector, Alexander McNair, Edward Bates.

County of Cooper: Robert Wallace and Robert P. Clarke.

County of St. Charles: Benjamin L. Emmons.

County of Washington: John Rice Jones.

County of St. Genevieve: Robert T. Brown, Henry Dodge and John Scott.

County of Madison: Nathaniel Cook.

County of Cape Girardeau: Joseph McFerron, Alexander Buckner.

County of Wayne: Elijah Bettis.

In addition to the Masonic delegates above named, William G. Pettus served as Secretary of the Convention.

The St. Louis delegates were members of Missouri Lodge No. 12, the Grand Lodge of Missouri not having been organized at the time. Wallace and Clark were members of Boonville Lodge No. 14; Emmons of St. Charles No. 28; Brown of Tucker No. 13; Dodge and Scott of Louisiana No. 109; Nathaniel Cook of Louisiana No. 109; McFerron of Western Star No. 107; Buckner of Unity No. 6; and Bettis of No. (?). (Listed in Washington Masonic circular of 1825).

Violette, in his story of the Convention, gives credit to Edward Bates, John Scott, John Rice Jones, John D. Cook and Jonathan S. Findlay, as the authors of the Constitution. The first three were members of the Craft. Tradition has named it the "Barton Constitution," probably because Barton was President of the Convention, for a close study of the Proceeding does not show undue activity on his part.

Brother Bates (later Grand Master) early in the session, offered a resolution to appoint a Committee of Three to draft a proposed Constitution; the delegates did not agree to his suggestion, but did adopt a resolution similar in character, whereby four committees of three delegates each were to draft parts of it. Those committees are here given with the Masonic names in italics:—

LEGISLATIVE	EXECUTIVE
John Rice Jones	*Wm. V. Rector*
Benjamin L. Emmons	John D. Cook
Robert P. Clarke	James Evans
JUDICIAL	BILL OF RIGHTS
Richard S. Thomas	Jonathan Ramsey
Nathaniel Cook	Samuel Hammond
Edward Bates	Duff Green

From this it can be seen that all of the members of the Legislative Committee were Craftsmen; Cook and Bates formed the majority of the Judicial Committee; Rector dominated the Executive Committee.

The Legislative Committee reported recommendations providing for a general assembly of two bodies, one representing the counties, the other representing the districts; membership was to be based on the population; all free male citizens above the age of 21 were given rights of citizenship, but no officer of the United States, priest or minister was to be eligible to position in the Legislature.

The Executive Committee set forth the various officers of the State Government, fixing their duration of office and salary, as well as manner of election and appointment.

The Judicial Committee created the various courts and provided for their election and appointment. The Committee on Bill of Rights recommended a guarantee of personal liberties as well as providing a schedule of changes necessary in changing from Territory to a State.

All of the reports of these Committees were received within two days following their assembly. *Without being read by the Convention* they were turned over to a select committee of four, denominated a Committee of a Whole, whose task was to put the four sections together as a complete whole. This Committee was headed by John Rice Jones, whose personality dominated the Committee, and who succeeded in incorporating many of his ideas in the draft, part of which he had already written as a member of the Legislative Committee. The new draft was submitted the following day.

Later, a Committee on Style was appointed, whose duty it was to rearrange the various sections as passed without in any manner changing their form or substance. Brother Bates headed this Committee; he was also made a member of the Committee on Engrossment and Enrollment.

A special Committee on Banks and Banking was appointed and this Committee included Thomas F. Riddick, whose practical experience in the Territorial Bank enabled him to introduce his ideas into the Committee report.

The most important committees were undoubtedly those on Style, the Committee on Banks, and the select Committee acting as a Committee of a Whole. Bates on the first named committee, Riddick on the second, and Jones on the latter gave to our fraternity ample representation. Jones and Bates were two of four men quoted by Violette as generally successful in having their views adopted.

When the election of a Secretary of the Convention was broached, the names of four Masons were presented, the vote being, William G. Pettus 21; Archibald Gamble 12; Thompson Douglass 3; Joseph V. Garnier 2.

The first act of the Convention, following its

official organization, was to take the oath to support the Constitution of the United States, the oath being administered by Brother Silas Bent, Judge of the Superior Court.

Emmons, Jones and Riddick were three of a committee appointed to draft rules for the government of the Convention, while Pratte and McNair were two of a committee of three to fit up and prepare the hall and rooms for the Convention and its committees. Accommodations were arranged for by John Rice Jones, who secured an agreement from Brother Wm. Bennett to provide the hall and two committee rooms at an expense of $30.00 for the week. Brother Wm. Rector of the Committee on Printing reported that they had consulted with a printer (Brother Isaac N. Henry) and by resolution moved that his offer be accepted.

The proposal of Brother Isaac N. Henry was unique; Henry will be remembered as the representative of Missouri Lodge No. 12 at the annual communication of the Grand Lodge of Tennessee in 1819.

St. Louis, June 14th, 1820.
To Messrs. Rector, Boone and Greene, committee for printing.
GENTLEMEN:
Your note of yesterday requesting to know the terms on which we would do such printing as the convention

should desire during its sitting, was duly received. We presume the printing you will require to be done, will principally consist of small jobs, we therefore propose to do it by the quire, at the same rates as we do blanks, viz, two dollars for each quire of paper that is made use of. The printing for the convention will be considerably more difficult to do than ordinary blanks, the above proposition is therefore something lower than we have been in the habit of printing for individual customers.

We are with respect your obedient servants,

Isaac N. Henry & Co.

Brother Henry later submitted a bid for printing twelve hundred copies of the Constitution and twelve hundred copies of the Journal at $100 for each job; his bid was accepted, although Brother Joseph Charless, a rival printer, had submitted bids through the President of the Convention.

A most unusual section was Section 9 of the Constitution; it had been presented originally by the Legislative Committee, Jones, Emmons and Clark, all of whom were Masons. The section read:

Section 9: No person while he continues to exercise the functions of a bishop, priest, clergyman, or teacher of any religious persuasion, denomination, society or sect whatever, shall be eligible to a seat in either branch of the legislature, or to be elected or appointed to any office of profit within the state, the office of justice of the peace excepted.

It is very evident that Emmons was not in harmony with the other two members of the committee which had presented the section, for when it was presented to the Convention for adoption, he promptly arose and moved to strike out the whole section. Thirty-nine votes were cast, 13 for striking it out and 26 for leaving it in; included in the 13 ayes were Brothers Emmons, McNair, McFerron, Bettis and Pratte; in the 26 nays were Brothers Bates, Clarke, Chouteau, Dodge, Jones, Rector, Riddick and Wallace.

A tribute was paid by the members of the Convention to a brother who was later to serve as Grand Master of Missouri in the following resolution:

> Resolved, that Nathaniel B. Tucker, Esq., late a judge of the circuit court, be admitted a seat within the hall of this Convention.

Brother John Rice Jones presented a second "religious section" known as Section 20; it read:

> Every gift, sale or devise of land to any minister, public teacher or preacher of the gospel as such, or to any religious sect, order or denomination, or to or for the support, use or benefit, of as such, or any religious order, sect or denomination; and every gift or sale of goods or chattels to go in

succession, or to take place after the death of the seller or donor, to or for such support, use or benefit; and also every devise of goods or chattels to or for the support, use or benefit of any minister, public teacher, or preacher of the gospel as such, or any religious order, or denomination, without leave of the general assembly shall be void, except always the sale, gift, lease or devise of any quantity of land not exceeding ten acres for a church, meeting or other house of worship and for a burying ground, which shall be improved, enjoyed or used only for such purposes or such sale, gift, lease or devise shall be void.

Three of the eight members voting for the adoption of the clause were Masons, Clarke, Jones and Riddick; ten Masons voted against it. Certainly the Masons of 1820 could not be accused by even their worst enemies of "religious intolerance."

Brother Bates then submitted a section in lieu of the one above, to read:

No religious corporation shall ever be established in this state.

There were 22 votes for its adoption, including 9 Masons while the 10 opposing votes, included 3 Masons, Brothers Bettis, McFerron and Pratte.

Several attempts were made to provide a law to do away with dueling; when first introduced, the section provided only that the general assembly might be given power to make laws for its suppression. This section was voted down by a large majority, although several Masons favored its adoption. Later on, the issue bobbed up again, this time in a remarkable form:

> The general assembly to suppress the evil practice of dueling, may pass laws to compel persons desirous of fighting duels, to fight unto death, in the presence and under the direction of a sworn officer, to be appointed for that purpose.

Brothers Bates, Buckner (who had fought a duel within the year), McFerron, and Pratte voted for this stringent section, the others opposing.

Brother John Scott was the father of the public school section (No. 35), beginning "schools and the means of education shall forever be encouraged in this state, and the general assembly shall take measures, etc., . . . shall be and remain a fund for the exclusive support of a state university, for the promotion of the arts, literature, and the sciences, etc." From this we might call Brother Scott the father of education in Missouri and the father of the university. Brother McFerron proposed an additional educational section, providing that "one or more schools shall be established in each township, so soon as practicable or necessary, under such rules and regulations as may be prescribed by law, and in such manner, . . . and that the poor may be taught gratis, but no particular dogmas of religion shall be inculcated at such schools."

When the Convention finally completed its work, a committee, consisting of Brothers Pratte, Chouteau and Riddick were appointed to translate the Constitution into French and distribute 300 copies. Brother McFerron was the only member of the Convention to vote "nay" on the final passage of the Constitution, even going so far as to have official protest made in the records of the last day:

> Mr. McFerron asked for and obtained leave to enter on the Journal, his protest which is in the following words, "Joseph McFerron a member of this Convention protests against the second section of the fourth article (the section had provided that the Governor should be a natural born citizen or a resident during a certain period) of this Constitution, for that it creates a distinction incompatible with the fact of citizenship, that it is repugnant to the principles of the Constitution of the United States, that it has a retrospective operation and degrades the naturalized citizen below the late subjects of the Spanish king, that it deprives such citizens of important vested rights of self government, and infringes that equality essential to the preservation of liberty, and which of right exists among all the parties to this Constitution, that it inverts the order of nature and raises the son above the father.

Thus Brother Joseph McFerron went down to defeat, but with banners flying.

Brother William G. Pettus, secretary, was charged with the responsibility of making up the journal of the Convention. By motion of Brother John Rice Jones, the Convention unanimously resolved that "the thanks of this Convention be bestowed on their secretary, for the faithful and correct manner in which he has performed the duties of his office."

The last official act was the motion of Brother Edward Bates to instruct the sergeant at arms to deliver the furniture of the Convention over to Jabez Warner (an applicant for degrees, refused admission because he was maimed).

In contrast to the expenses of later Conventions, was the $26.25 expense reported by Brother Pettus, the secretary, for ink, paper, stationery, books, etc., used by the Convention. The entire work was accomplished in one month and put into effect without a vote of the people. It was necessary that the Constitution be engrossed on parchment, an act which was completed over night in the copperplate handwriting of Brother Pettus, which prompted a member of the Convention to say on the floor of the Convention:

It has been enrolled on parchment by your secretary, and permit me, Mr. President, to add that my business has been for many years to read proof-sheets, having been a newspaper editor, and I am free to say that I never saw such a paper as this. There is not an interlineation; there is not one word misspelled, there is not an "t" uncrossed nor an "i" undotted in the whole instrument, and as such, as chairman of the committee, I present it to the Convention for signatures.

A great compliment to a Brother Master Mason!

Things moved swiftly from the date of the closing of the Convention; August 28, 1820, an election was held for State officers; two Master Masons opposed each other in the contest for Governor, Brother Alexander McNair and Brother William Clark, the latter at the time Governor of the Territory. McNair went into office by a large majority. Brother Nathaniel Cook was defeated for Lieutenant Governor by General Wm. Ashley, there being three candidates in the field. Brother John Scott, then Territorial Delegate, was elected to the sixteenth and seventeenth Congresses.

John Rice Jones was the leading member of the Convention; he had passed three score years, possessed an education and training superior to those of his fellow-delegates, speaking French, Spanish, and English with equal facility and with a personality as a speaker which rendered him almost invincible. Barton was, no doubt, the popular idol of the day, but his morals, his habits, and his education did not place him in the same category as Jones, Bates and one or two others.

Governor McNair began his administration by naming three Master Masons to the five appointive positions allowed him; they were: Brother William G. Pettus, private secretary; Brother Edward Bates, Attorney-General; Brother Wm. Christy, Auditor of Accounts.

The Legislature met in St. Louis for its first session, Monday, September 18, 1820, in the old Missouri Hotel, southwest corner of Main and Morgan Streets. Brother John McArthur was made clerk of the House, and Brother Silas Bent presided as President *pro tem* of the Senate. Brother Thomas H. Benton was one of the two Senators selected to represent the new State in the National Senate at Washington; the deciding vote was cast by John Ralls, father of Colonel John Ralls, Grand Master of Missouri in 1849; it was the last act of Ralls, who was carried in his bed from his room to the Convention floor, his death occurring a few hours later. They were admitted to seats after Brother McNair had convened a special session of the legislature at St. Charles, June 4, 1821, for the purpose of repealing some obnoxious clauses, and on August 10, 1821, President and Brother James Monroe issued his proclamation, declaring the admission of Missouri as the twenty-fourth State in the National Union.

Seventeen years had passed since Missouri Territory had been acquired by the United States; these years had been full of wonderful accomplishments. From a motley cluster of dingy settlements there had grown up towns of considerable distinction and the State now possessed a population of more than 60,000. Those who had received Masonic light were in no small way responsible for these successes.

CHAPTER XIV

THE FIRST GRAND LODGE IN MISSOURI TERRITORY

IN 1820, the year previous to the formation of the Grand Lodge of Missouri (the first to be composed of lodges existing west of the Mississippi River), there had been chartered, or were waiting for charters, since the transfer of the Territory in 1804, the following lodges:

LOUISIANA LODGE No. 107, warrant ordered issued by the Grand Lodge of Pennsylvania on July 17, 1807. It did not become a member of the Grand Lodge of Missouri, although conferred degrees as late as 1821.

ST. LOUIS LODGE No. 111, warrant ordered issued September 15, 1808, by the Grand Lodge of Pennsylvania; Lodge never made returns and forfeited charter, the members forming,

MISSOURI LODGE No. 12, under the Grand Lodge of Tennessee, the most active Masonically of all the Lodges in the Valley; this Lodge was authorized by Dispensation from the Grand Lodge of Tennessee, October 3, 1815.

JOACHIM LODGE No. 25, located at Herculaneum, Missouri, Dispensation having been authorized by the Grand Lodge of Tennessee, January 4, 1819.

ST. CHARLES LODGE No. 28, authorized by the Grand Lodge of Tennessee, July 5, 1819, located at St. Charles, Missouri.

THE FIRST GRAND LODGE IN MISSOURI

POTOSI LODGE No. 39, chartered in 1816 by the Grand Lodge of Kentucky, but which lasted but two years.

UNITY LODGE, U. D., Dispensation issued by the Grand Lodge of Indiana, through its Grand Master, December 21, 1820.

A number of Masons living in and near Louisiana, Missouri, had gone so far towards organizing a lodge, as to prepare a petition, which was forwarded to the Grand Lodge of Tennessee, asking for a dispensation; this organization later became Harmony Lodge No. 4.

Missouri No. 12, Joachim No. 25, St. Charles No. 28, and Unity, U. D. were the only lodges from which a Grand Lodge could be formed, and their total membership included less than 100 members. What a wonderful prospect for a Grand Lodge! No money, no members, and but four lodges, one of which was under dispensation! But our brethren of one hundred years ago did not have to support an expensive organization, the Grand Secretary was satisfied with $10 annual salary; they had not begun to build the George Washington Memorial, they had no conception of an Educational or Service Association, the only Board of Relief they knew functioned by reaching down in the pocket to relieve the distress of a worthy brother, his widow and orphan; and official visitations, district deputies and the laying of cornerstones were far from their thoughts!

Brethren who had left the comforts of an Eastern civilization to make their homes, in what, only a few years previous, had been a trackless wilderness, were not to be dismayed by the lack of such mere trifles as numbers or finance. Accounts are extremely rare, especially at that time, of Grand Lodges organized with as few as three legitimate chartered lodges—but then, these were Missourians! Had not Louisiana organized a Grand Lodge in 1812, Indiana in 1818, Kentucky in 1800 and Tennessee in 1813? Why not, then, Missouri, which had this year entered the great sisterhood of States?

There were real reasons, however, for the organization of a Grand Lodge in Missouri; in the first place, Missouri was a legal entity, a sovereign State; as such, the lodges in this State believed themselves entitled to assume the legal powers of a Grand Lodge.

Secondly, three of the lodges then at work were daughters of the Grand Lodge of Tennessee, the other, of the Grand Lodge of Indiana. Masonry of every State was represented among the pioneers who made up the lodges in Missouri; unification of work demanded a strong central organization which would standardize the ritual. Again, the matter of representation in Grand Lodge was a potent factor in forcing actions. The distance to Tennessee or Indiana was too great, in the days of poor transportation, to permit the lodges to be represented at the Annual Communication, and without this personal contact, lodges did not thrive or receive the inspiration necessary to make them successful. The danger attached to communication by letter, or the transmission of money by mails, was an additional reason. And then, there was probably that other reason, not usually mentioned except in a low breath— the desire to be a Grand Officer—and very few of the membership had ever seen such an official!

The leading officers in Missouri Lodge No. 12 were undoubtedly responsible for the preliminary steps taken; invitations were sent to the surrounding lodges asking them to meet in a preliminary convention on February 22, 1821, for the purpose of organizing a Grand Lodge. It is very doubtful if such an invitation was sent to any lodges but Nos. 25 and 28.

Accordingly, there assembled in the hall of Missouri Lodge No. 12, on Elm Street, between Main and Second Streets, on the date mentioned, representatives from the three lodges under Tennessee charter. The only brethren known to participate in this Convention were:

MISSOURI No. 12: Edward Bates, Wm. Renshaw.
JOACHIM No. 25: William Bates.
ST. CHARLES No. 28: Nathaniel Simonds.

Edward Bates, then Master of No. 12, presided and was made permanent chairman of the meeting. William Renshaw was made secretary, presumably because of his residence in St. Louis, while Edward Bates was the most prominent of those present, and naturally fitted for chairman. Very little was accomplished at this time except to frame some resolutions (preparatory to withdrawal from the Mother Grand Lodge), which were to be referred to each of the lodges represented in the Convention.

The following preamble and resolution was adopted:

Whereas, the subordinate Lodges of this State are situated at a considerable distance from the Grand Lodges by which they have been severally chartered, and their attendance upon the Grand Lodges to which they are subordinate, is rendered inconvenient and expensive, and whereas Masonry is daily increasing, and the number of Lodges multiplying in this State——

Therefore—1st. Be it Resolved, That it is expedient and necessary to the interest of the Craft that a Grand Lodge should be established in this State to be invested with all the powers and privileges usually enjoyed by Grand Lodges heretofore established.

2d. Be it Resolved, That a Committee of three be appointed to draft a Constitution for the government of the Grand Lodge so to be established, and that they send a copy thereof to each of the Lodges in this State within two weeks from this date.

3d. Be it Resolved, That each of the Lodges in this State, be requested, as soon as conveniently may be, after receiving a copy of the Constitution, as provided for in the second resolution, to pass upon the same, and decide whether they will ratify or reject it, and whether they will voluntarily place themselves under the jurisdiction of the Grand Lodge so to be established; and further that they be requested, with as little delay as possible, to communicate their proceedings thereon to all the Lodges in this State.

4th. Be it Resolved, That if a majority of the Lodges in this State do ratify such Constitution, and do agree to place themselves under the jurisdiction of such Grand Lodge, the officers of such Lodges, by themselves or their proxies, properly appointed, and all Past Masters usually admitted to seats in Grand Lodges, shall meet in the town of St. Louis, on the 23rd day of April, A. L. 5821, and there organize the Grand Lodge, and elect the necessary officers.

5th. Be it Resolved, That Brothers Wm. Bates, of Joachim Lodge No. 25, Nathaniel Simonds of St. Charles Lodge No. 28, and Edward Bates of Missouri Lodge No. 12, be appointed a committee to draft a Constitution of the Grand Lodge, in pursuance of the second resolution.

6th. Be it Resolved, That a copy of these resolutions be sent to each of the Lodges in this State.

Attest: EDWARD BATES, Presiding.
    WM. RENSHAW, *Secretary.*

It is highly probable that the above preamble and resolutions were largely the work of Edward Bates, the dominant character in the Committee as well as in the Convention itself. Only a few months before he had taken a leading part in the making of a State Constitution for Missouri, although he was next the youngest member of the State Convention; a remarkable and virile personality.

Briefly, the Constitution, as prepared by this Committee, provided for the officers of the Grand Lodge (practically the same as now), and gave a name to the Grand Lodge, "The Grand Lodge of Missouri, of Ancient, Free and Accepted Masons." Semi-Annual Communications were provided for, with a provision for Emergent Communications when necessary. Methods of representation, manner of election of officers, powers of the Grand Lodge, finances, and a few other minor matters were set forth, and the whole report signed by the Committee. The one section which proved a stumbling block for many years, was the method of amending the Constitution; it provided that all amendments after being proposed in Grand Lodge should be submitted for a referendum vote to the various lodges, when, if two-thirds had ratified them, they were to become a part of the Constitution.

THE FIRST GRAND LODGE IN MISSOURI 253

Two months later (April 23, 1821) the delegates again assembled to consider the results of their February Convention; Edward Bates presided, but the representatives of but two lodges appeared and an adjournment was taken until the following day at three o'clock, when it was hoped that St. Charles Lodge might be represented. The April 23 meeting was attended by Edward Bates, James Kennerly, William Bates, Abraham Beck, Joseph V. Garnier, Isaac A. Letcher, Joseph White, John C. Potter, John Jones, J—— Craig, Thornton Grimsley, W. H. Pocock, James H. Penrose, Wm. G. Pettus, W. H. Hopkins, and H—— Hardin.

Abraham Platt of St. Charles Lodge appeared on the following afternoon; Edward Bates and John D. Daggett appeared for Missouri No. 12, and William Bates for Joachim No. 25, whereupon Bates proceeded to open the Convention with the assistance of Brothers James Kennerly, Abraham Beck, William G. Pettus, George H. C. Melody, John C. Potter, Hugh Rankin, Harvey Hunt, Thompson Douglass and Thos. F. Riddick. All Past Masters were by resolution given the right of ballot, whereupon an election was held, the following Grand Officers were elected and the new Grand Lodge of Missouri came into being.

Thomas Fiveash Riddick, *Grand Master*
James Kennerly, *Senior Grand Warden*
William Bates, *Junior Grand Warden*
Archibald Gamble, *Grand Treasurer*
William Renshaw, *Grand Secretary*

Adjournment was had until Friday, May 4, 1821, when:

Brother Douglass having been requested by the Most Worshipful Grand Master elect, to officiate, for the purpose of consecrating and installing the Grand Officers of this new Grand Lodge, a procession was formed and proceeded to the Baptist Church, where the solemn ceremony of consecration and installation was performed in conformity with the ancient landmarks and customs of the fraternity. Procession again formed and returned to the Lodge-room.

The Grand Master appointed John W. Honey and John Jones as Deacons and they were installed, in addition to the ones elected April 24, 1821. Almost half the entire membership of the Craft in Missouri were present at the installation, and on their return to the lodge-room, Worshipful Brother Edward Bates proposed that a Committee be appointed to draft a code of by-laws for the government of the Grand Lodge; Douglass, Pettus and Garnier were appointed. The Resolution of February 22, 1821, came up for ratification, which having been accomplished, an adjournment was had until the following day, when the Com-

THE FIRST GRAND LODGE IN MISSOURI

mittee on By-Laws made their report, which was adopted.

A provision was enacted whereby those lodges comprising the Grand Lodge might surrender their charters and receive one from the Grand Lodge of Missouri. Under this regulation, the following lodges were issued charters by the Grand Lodge:

>   *Missouri No.* 1; (formerly No. 12)
>   *Joachim No.* 2; (formerly No. 25)
>   *Hiram No.* 3; (formerly No. 28)

The first act of the new Grand Master was to issue a dispensation to the members of Harmony Lodge No. 4, at Louisiana, Missouri, August 10, 1821. Unity Lodge, U. D., at Jackson petitioned for a charter, but the Grand Lodge very wisely side-stepped issuing a charter until Unity had been given official release by the Grand Lodge of Indiana. In the meantime, Olive Branch Lodge at Alton appeared for charter and Unity was compelled to receive the number "6" although as a matter of right was probably entitled to No. "4."

The total receipts of the Grand Lodge for the first year amounted to $96.50 exclusive of charity funds; the Grand Lodge, however, having gone to some expense, appropriating the following:

James D. Daggett, seal	$20.00
Wm. Orr, printing proceedings	20.00
Essex and Hough, charters, etc.	22.50
John C. Potter, Grand Tiler	10.00
Wm. Renshaw, Grand Secretary	20.00
Contingent expenses	50.00

These amounts total $142.50 which was $46 more than the Most Worshipful Grand Lodge collected, but it is presumed that the M. W. G. L. believed in dealing in "futures," or that it were possible to make a raid on the "Grand Charity Fund" then consisting of $19.75.

No statistics are furnished in any of the reports made by the Grand Lodge; however, the Charity Fund gives a clue as to the probable membership at the close of the first year. The By-Laws provided that 25c per capita tax should be collected annually to go into the Charity Fund. Working on this basis we are able to arrive at the total membership in Missouri, as follows:

From	Amount	Members
Missouri No. 1	$10.25	41
Joachim No. 2	3.75	15
Hiram No. 3	3.00	12
Harmony No. 4	2.50	10
	$19.75	78

It would seem that the Grand Lodge was losing membership since its formation, but the seeming troubles of 1821 were as naught compared with those then unforeseen, which were to follow in less than a decade, troubles which were fanned to fever heat by intolerance, bigotry, superstition and jealousy. We can go no further with the story at this time; we have shown how the Grand Lodge was organized, some of the problems it had to meet, and the legal maze necessary for it to pass through. It remains now to chronicle something concerning that most distinguished citizen, whose task it was to assume the wheel of the new ship and to steer it across an uncharted sea, a brother to whom the fraternity will ever be indebted, and a citizen whose name should be imprinted in the hearts of every Missouri child, as the father of the public school system in Missouri—Thomas Fiveash Riddick—first Grand Master of the Grand Lodge, Ancient Free and Accepted Masons of Missouri.

Masonic historians wander in a mystic maze when discussing the Masonic record of our first Grand Master. He was a member of Solomon Lodge No. 30, in Suffolk, Virginia; from the time of his arrival in St. Louis, shortly after the transfer of the Territory, he showed himself an ardent Freemason. He visited Western

Star Lodge at Kaskaskia, Illinois, sixty miles away, before a lodge had been chartered west of the Mississippi River; the records show him there on at least two occasions, March 24, 1806, and December 27, 1806.

On the latter date, he signed a petition for a new lodge to be known as Louisiana Lodge to be located at St. Genevieve, Missouri; this would lead us to believe the St. Genevieve petition was prepared and circulated at the St. John the Evangelist meeting in Kaskaskia, in 1806. However, when the new lodge was constituted, Riddick was not a member, it being plainly evident that he signed only to assist his St. Genevieve brethren in securing their dispensation.

In the application for a dispensation for St. Louis Lodge No. 111 prepared for submission to the Grand Lodge of Pennsylvania, his is the second name, following directly after that of the Governor of the Territory, Meriwether Lewis. The application includes the recommendation that he be made the first Senior Warden of the new lodge. He was installed in the position by Captain and Judge Otho Shrader, November 8, 1808.

He was present at the conferring of the degrees on General William Clark, in September 1809, serving as Senior Warden, while the illus-

THE FIRST GRAND LODGE IN MISSOURI

trious Frederick Bates presided as Master (Bates was the second Governor of Missouri). He later became a charter member of Missouri Lodge No. 12, and later of Missouri No. 1, having been a charter member of three lodges in Missouri under three separate jurisdictions.

At the formation of the Grand Lodge of Missouri, he is not noted as a member or visitor until the day of the election, April 24, 1821, when he appeared as a spectator, and by virtue of a resolution granting the right of ballot to all Past Masters, he became a member of the Grand Lodge. His popularity caused him to be selected as the first Grand Master and he was installed as such May 4, 1821, filling the position with dignity and honor. Following the collapse of his bank in 1822, he moved to Sulphur Springs, Jefferson County, Missouri, where he died at the early age of forty-nine, on January 15, 1830, leaving a widow, two sons and two daughters. He is last mentioned in the report of Missouri Lodge No. 1, in the year 1826; he is never thereafter mentioned as a member, as died, dimitted or suspended.

Colonel Thomas Fiveash Riddick was the son of Thomas Riddick and Fanny Fiveash, born in the town of Suffolk, Nansemond County, Virginia, June 5, 1781, arriving in the Territory about 1804. While a resident of St. Louis he filled many positions of honor and distinction; he was one of the most active and influential business men of his home city and was always found among those working for the public betterment.

In 1807, he was appointed by Frederick Bates, then Secretary of the Treasury, as assessor of rates and levies for the district of St. Louis. The same year he was given another appointment by Bates; a Clerk of the Court of Common Pleas Quarter Sessions and Oyer and Terminer for the district of St. Louis; the same year he was made a Justice of the Peace. In 1808, he was appointed by his friend Bates to represent him as Recorder of Land Titles, during his absence from St. Louis on official business. In 1812, Bates reappointed him as Justice of the Peace, and in 1813, he was reappointed to the other positions which he was then filling. January 2, 1815, General William Clark named him a Justice of the Peace and in 1817 he became one of the first directors in the Territorial Bank of Missouri, succeeding Col. Auguste Chouteau as President in 1820, a position he was holding at the time of his election as Grand Master.

The collapse of the bank in 1822 caused great concern to Colonel Riddick. The Bank had been incorporated by the Territorial Legislature, December 17, 1816, but in anticipation of the act the bank had actually begun to function September 30, 1816, having built a banking house at No. 6 North Main Street. In this venture with Riddick were associated a number of other well-known characters and Brother Masons; of these, Senator Thomas H. Benton, Thomas Brady and James Kennerly were probably best known. Riddick had also been instrumental in the organization of an earlier bank in 1813, known as the Bank of St. Louis, which suffered the same fate as the Bank of Missouri at about the same time the latter bank was starting (1819). The earlier bank contained more Masonic names than did the later one; among the incorporators, we note Bernard Pratte, Thomas Brady, Bartholomew Berthold, Rufus Easton, Risdon H. Price; later are recorded the names of Riddick, Wm. Rector, Joshua Pilcher, Thompson Douglass and others.

Riddick was an honest and competent business official, and the failure of the bank was in no way due to bad management, but largely to the unsettled condition existing at the time.

At the first session of the Territorial Legislature in 1812, Riddick was elected Clerk *pro tem;* in 1818 we find him representing St.

Louis in the fourth and last of the Territorial Legislatures. Encouraged by his political success, Riddick aspired to a seat in Congress; he made a race in 1814 against two other Masons, Rufus Easton and Alexander McNair, running a poor third.

During the Black Hawk War, Riddick enlisted as a Major in command of the first battalion organized in St. Louis under Colonel Alexander McNair.

Riddick believed Freemasonry to be the handmaiden of the church and was an ardent churchman; he was affiliated with the Episcopalian denomination, which was not represented in the Territory until 1819, when the Reverend John Ward of Lexington, Kentucky, (Grand Chaplain of the Grand Lodge of Kentucky in 1822) came to St. Louis and preached a sermon to the resident members, Sunday October 7, 1819, in the old Baptist Church, Third and Market Streets. The visit of Reverend Ward inspired those of that faith with new hopes, so much so that Colonel Riddick summoned all Episcopalians interested to meet at his office, Monday, December 6, 1819, for the purpose of holding an election of Wardens and Vestrymen for the proposed congregation, about to be established under the name of Christ Church, the name borne at this day. The election resulted in the selection of the following members of the Masonic fraternity: Thomas F. Riddick, Warden; Joseph V. Garnier, Robert Wash, William Rector, James Kennerly, and five others, of whose membership we are still in doubt.

Reverend Ward was engaged as a permanent rector, his sermon of October 7, 1819, no doubt, being a trial sermon. Previous to the election of officers in 1819, Colonel Riddick took charge of the circulation of a subscription list to raise funds for the support of the church; he was a believer in practicing what he preached and his name led the rest with a subscription of $100, a total of $1714 being subscribed, no small amount for that day. The immediate result was the organization of Christ Church, the third of the Protestant organizations to be formed in St. Louis.

Grand Master Riddick was a true American citizen, exemplifying in his daily life the Masonic virtues. In 1819, when President James Monroe planned a visit to the West, with the expectation of including St. Louis in his itinerary, a meeting of citizens was called to consider plans for his entertainment. The meeting was held June 9, 1819, in Colonel Riddick's auction-house. In 1818 the Fourth of July was observed by the citizens of St. Louis, the Declaration of Independence being read by Colonel Riddick, who possessed a strong, clear voice.

In 1818 he was one of the subscribers to a fund for the erection of a public theater, a venture which did not prove financially successful. His advertisement appeared in the papers at the time, examples of which are:

June 18, 1816:
> Thomas F. Riddick, Auctioneer.

November 30, 1816:
> Riddick and Pilcher.

Auctioneers, South Main, a new frame warehouse in rear for storage.

May 30, 1820:
> Riddick and Honey,

Auctioneers, at Riddicks old stand.

The Pilcher mentioned was Major Joshua Pilcher, member of Missouri No. 12, and a relative of Colonel Riddick. John W. Honey, also mentioned as a partner, was a Mason and also a relative (a step-brother of Riddick) who married in 1810, Marie Antoinette, daughter of Sylvestre Labadie.

The old Riddick Mansion, built of brick, was one of the show places of St. Louis; Colonel Riddick's residence, on the west side of South Fourth Street, opposite Plum Street, in 1818 was regarded as well out in the country. The dimensions of the house are given as 36 feet front by 18 feet in depth, two rooms above and two below. One of the novelties introduced in the building were window panes 13x18 inches, "extra large size" imported from Pittsburg. In this building Colonel Riddick made his home until 1823 when it was purchased and used as a public resort known as Vaux Hall Garden.

His last recorded Masonic appearance was when he accompanied the Grand Lodge, August 31, 1823, for the purpose of laying the cornerstone of the first Presbyterian Church erected west of the Mississippi River; the Grand Lodge met in the hall of Missouri Lodge No. 1 and marched in procession to the site of the new church, north-west corner of Fourth and St. Charles, a location at that time somewhat remote from the center of population.

The greatest work done by Colonel Riddick was with the land titles of property in the Territory, which resulted in the securing of a magnificent fund for the support of the public school system. Following the transfer of government in 1804, the United States found itself confronted with the problem of confirming all the land grants made by the French and Spanish governments which had owned the

Territory. Titles had been poorly recorded, for several reasons, probably the best of which was the lack of survey, and again, poor facilities for recording land grants. To complicate matters, the New Madrid earthquake grants entered into the trouble, and forgeries, fake claims, and land speculators made land claims produce pangs of fear in more than one breast. So strong was the influence of the land speculator that it even extended into the halls of Congress itself.

In June 1812 Congress passed an act providing for the confirmation of titles in the Territory, and setting forth that all unclaimed lands were to be reserved for the support of the public schools; the amount which fell to the city of St. Louis from this act was almost three hundred acres, which in the first annual report of the St. Louis public schools was estimated at almost half a million dollars and by 1876 at more than a million dollars.

Evidence of the part played in the securing of this magnificent endowment is furnished by the local historian, Colonel John F. Darby in his Recollections of November 15, 1876:

> The value of these lands now owned by the schools, in round numbers, may be stated to be today a million and a half dollars. The second section of this law, giving these lands to the public schools, was inserted in the act by Mr.

THE FIRST GRAND LODGE IN MISSOURI

Hempstead (Representative in Congress) *at the special and earnest request of Colonel Thomas F. Riddick,* who knew all about the town, and knew that there were certain lots of ground in the town for which no rightful owners or claimants could be found, *and with him originated the idea* of giving these lots not rightfully claimed, to the public schools. And for this purpose Colonel Riddick started on horseback and rode all the way to Washington City *and at his own individual expense,* to have this desirable object consummated and carried out, which was done. Of these things I have heard from Colonel Riddick himself; and afterwards from Archibald Gamble, Esq., so long the efficient and active agent of the public schools in looking after their interest in these lands, informed me that to Colonel Riddick was due the credit of having this grant of lands made, and which Mr. Hempstead carried through Congress.

For this great and valuable inheritance now enjoyed by the schools, Colonel Riddick deserves to have a monument erected to his memory. It was my good fortune to know Colonel Riddick intimately and well. I had visited at his house, and have shared the generous hospitality of his domicile, and have received the warm, friendly greeting of his friendship and that of the whole family. Colonel Riddick was among the very first trustees of the public schools. He was a member of the Convention that formed the first Constitution of the State of Missouri, being elected on the same ticket from the County of St. Louis with such men as Edward Bates, Governor McNair, General Bernard Pratte, and Pierre Chouteau, Jr., (all Freemasons). When he embarked in any measure, he was one of the most enthusiastic men that have ever lived in this town; he died beloved by all and honored and respected by all who knew him. It is with the most becoming and deference of respect towards the members of the Board of the St. Louis Public Schools, that I may be permitted to express the hope, that the Board will before long, take some suitable action to erect a proper monument to the memory of one who has conferred upon them the means of doing so much good, and from which those under their charge have been blessed with and have derived such lasting benefits. In fact so far as the St. Louis Public Schools are concerned, Colonel Thomas F. Riddick, was the creator and originator of that noble system of instruction in St. Louis.

This worthy citizen, who had labored so hard for his community, was finally to sacrifice the small amount of personal fortune which he had succeeded in accumulating, in an unsuccessful business enterprise. He had taken literally the injunction given him during his early Masonic career in respect to his three great duties "to God, his neighbor, and himself." He had shown himself active in the church of God by implanting the first church of his faith in the Territory; he had respected the rights of his neighbor in all things, and had encouraged the great system of Public Schools which were to benefit his lesser favored neighbors; and finally, he was himself a model citizen, friendly, warm-hearted, generous, patriotic, decent and respectable.

Where in all of Louisiana Territory could the Masonic fraternity have gone to discover one more fitted to be the first in all its history, to wear the title of First Grand Master, of the Grand Lodge of Ancient Free and Accepted Masons of Missouri, the first Grand Lodge West of the Mississippi River?

From this time on the story of Freemasonry in the West becomes one in which many states are to be considered, for the period of statehood had begun. It would be interesting to go further, for the Masonic story of the Santa Fé and Oregon Trails, the Mormon settlements, the Mexican and Civil War periods, and later events, is one to thrill the heart of every red-blooded member of the fraternity, as he learns of the bravery, the prowess, and the hardships of his pioneer brother, in his effort to make a home for himself and those who might follow after him.

Some day, some member of the Craft will tell us of this most interesting period; for the present, we have at least builded a foundation for the writer who may follow. And, if the reader has found herein a few moments of enjoyment and satisfaction, if he feels that such a story should be permanently recorded, then the writer can believe that his labor has not been in vain.

INDEX

Alexander, Walter B., received degrees in Missouri No. 12, 190

Allen, William, organizer of Harmony No. 4, 223; Grand Master of Kentucky Grand Lodge, 198.

American Fur Co., foundation of, 26; in the Louisiana Territory, 4.

American Philosophical Society, asked to secure explorer, 19.

Andrews, Thomas, member St. Louis No. 20; received degrees in Missouri No. 12, 190.

Arundel, William, organizer of Western Star, 96; received diploma from Western Star, 111.

Arkansas, creation of District, 12.

Ash, G. W., probably member of St. Charles No. 28, 212.

Ashley, William, first Lieut. Governor of Missouri, 243; attacked by Indians, 25; fur trading with Indians, 25.

Austin, Stephen F., military service of, 63; member Louisiana No. 109, 168.

Bache, Richard, member Committee on By-Laws of Louisiana No. 109, 147.

Baker, George A., Jr., on Committee on By-Laws of Louisiana No. 109, 147; Grand Secretary of Pennsylvania Grand Lodge, 98.

Barber, Horace, probably member of St. Charles No. 28, 212.

Bartholomew, Joseph, active in Freemasonry in Indiana, 204; organizer of Vincennes Lodge, 69; Senior Grand Warden Indiana Grand Lodge, 69; wounded at Tippecanoe, 69.

Bates, Edward, acting Governor of Missouri, 72; member Cabinet of Pres. Lincoln, 4; delegate to Missouri State Convention, 232; first Attorney General of Missouri, 55, 244; member first State Legislature, 55; offered post as Secretary of War by Fillmore, 55; on Judicial Committee of State Constitution, 233; organizer Grand Lodge of Missouri, 251; presided at Whig Convention, 55; received degrees in Missouri No. 12, 190; studied law in St. Louis, 54; U. S. Attorney General under Lincoln, 55; U. S. District Attorney for Missouri, 55.

Bates, Frederick, compiler "Laws of the Territory of Louisiana," 12; Governor of Missouri, 187; member Missouri No. 12, 189; Master St. Louis No. 111, 12; Secretary and acting Governor Louisiana Territory, 12.

Bates, Robert, received degrees in Unity No. 6, 229.

Bates, William, death of, 222; Junior Grand Warden of Missouri Grand Lodge, 221, 254; Junior Warden Joachim No. 25, 220; member Louisiana No. 109, 168; organizer Grand Lodge of Missouri, 250.

Beaumont, James S., member Joachim No. 25, 221.

Beck, Abraham, organizer Missouri Grand Lodge, 253; member Missouri No. 12, 190.

Beck, Lewis C., settled in Missouri, 40.

Beckes, Benjamin, first white child born in Indiana Territory, 69.

Beckes, Parmenas, first Mason created in Indiana, 79; killed in duel with Dr. Scull, 79; served at Tippecanoe, 69.

Bennett, William, owner of Mansion House, St. Louis, 231.

Bent, Charles, Masonic membership of, 50; opener of Great Southwest, 23.

Bent, Silas, administered oath to Missouri State Convention, 236; Clerk of County Court, 49; deputy surveyor, 49; Judge Common Pleas, 49, 72, 187; Masonic membership, 50, 187; pioneer in legal profession, 49; President pro tem. first Missouri Senate, 244.

Benton, Thomas Hart, duel with Lucas, 29, 84; editor of "The Enquirer," 58; famous in Louisiana Territory, 4; first U. S. Senator from Missouri, 244; member Missouri No. 12, 189; military service, 63; quarrel with Andrew Jackson, 56, 82; prominent in Missouri politics, 56; author "Thirty Years in the Senate," 36, 56; U. S. Senator, 56.

Berry, Taylor, duel with Abiel Leonard, 54; military service, 54.

Berry, Thomas, received degrees in Missouri No. 12, 191.

Berthold, Bartholomew, business enterprises, 26; carried Masonic funds to Philadelphia, 153; death of, 27; member Louisiana No. 109, 26, 168; organized first Territorial Bank, 26; pioneer in Louisiana Territory, 4; settled in Mississippi Valley, 26.

Bettis, Elijah, delegate Missouri State Convention, 232.

Bibb, Richard G., member Louisiana No. 109, 168.

Bible Society, Kentucky, founded, 198.

Billon, Charles F., member St. Louis No. 111, 188.

Bird, G. A., member Louisiana No. 109, 162.

Blanchard, George, received degrees in Missouri No. 12, 191.

Bond, Shadrach, first Governor of Illinois, 88, 207; first Grand Master Illinois Grand Lodge, 88, 207; first Illinois Territorial delegate to Congress, 207; member General Assembly of Illinois, 207; Receiver Public Moneys, 208; secured act encouraging immigration, 208; visited Western Star, 99.

Boon, Hampton, early minister in Missouri, 61.

Boss, Daniel C., member Missouri No. 12, 190.

Bossier, John B., member Louisiana No. 109, 168.

Brady, James G., member Louisiana No. 109, 168.

Brady, Thomas, chairman Erin Benevolent Society, 73; or-

INDEX

ganizer of Missouri No. 12, 188.

Bridger, James, experiences as trapper, 30.

Brown, Robert T., delegate Missouri State Convention, 232; member Louisiana No. 109, 168.

Bruce, Amos J., officer "St. Louis Guards," 64; received degrees in Missouri No. 12, 190.

Bruer, Richard, organizer Harmony No. 4, 223.

Bruff, Major J., commandant of Upper Louisiana Territory, 62; organizer St. Louis No. 111, 170, 172; made first written record of Royal Arch Masonry in Louisiana Territory, 63; Masonic membership, 63; military service of, 62.

Buckner, Alexander, delegate Missouri State Convention, 232; engaged in law practice, 45; first Grand Master Indiana Grand Lodge, 44, 204; fought duel with Col. Blake, 86; Master Unity No. 6, 228; organizer Grand Lodge of Indiana, 45; organizer Unity No. 6, 204, 227; memorial at Cape Girardeau, 44; public offices held by, 45; Senator from Missouri, 44; settled in Missouri, 45.

Bullitt, George, Junior Warden Louisiana No. 109, 155; Junior Warden St. Louis No. 111, 173; member Territorial Legislature, 45; one of first petitioners Western Star Lodge, 99; organizer Louisiana No. 109, 122, 149; organizer Unity No. 6, 227; Register of Land Office, 45.

Buntin, Thomas, Sr., account of battlefield at Fort Washington, 65.

Burr, Aaron, attempt to found new kingdom, 14; Masonic membership, 100; visited Western Star, 100.

Burtscher, Sebastian, member Louisiana No. 109, 158, 168.

Bynum, Grey, first teacher in Howard Co., Mo., 60.

Cabanne, John, member of American Fur Co., 27.

Cabbeen, William, member Louisiana No. 109, 168.

California, early lodges in, 17.

Carr, William C., came to St. Louis in keel boat, 49; engaged in law practice in St. Louis, 49; Masonic membership, 49; organizer newspaper, 58.

Carson, Kit, exploits of, 4; scout and explorer, 23.

Carson, Moses B., Masonic membership, 30; organizer Missouri Fur Co., 29.

Carter, John R., organizer Harmony No. 4, 223.

Cass, Lewis, application for Masonic membership, 204; elected to Legislature, 205; first Grand Master of Michigan, 205; Governor of Territory, 205; Grand Master of Ohio, 204; inquired into Aaron Burr conspiracy, 205; Minister to France, 205; Presidential candidate, 206; Secretary of State under Buchanan, 206; Secretary of War under Jackson, 206; served in War of 1812, 205; settled in Ohio, 205; U. S. Marshal, 205; U. S. Senator, 206.

Cellinger, Henry, in Joachim No. 25, 221.

Chambers, A. B., Grand Master of Missouri Grand Lodge, 184; Master of St. Louis No. 20, 183.

Charless, Joseph, first newspaper editor in Missouri, 57; member of St. Louis No. 111, 188; organizer Erin Benevolent Society, 74; Masonic history of, 58; printed first book in Territory, 12, 58; rival newspaper organized, 58.

Cheatham, Edward, member Louisiana No. 109, 168.

Chouteau, Pierre, Jr., Assistant Judge Common Pleas, 72; captain of troop of horse in militia, 64; delegate Missouri State Convention, 232; fur prince, 27; in the development of the Louisiana Territory, 4; joined Missouri Fur Co., 24; member St. Louis No. 111, 188; military service of, 63; organizer St. Louis No. 111, 170; prominent in St. Louis, 27; treaty with Assiniboine and Blackfeet Indians, 28.

Christ Church, St. Louis, organized by Freemasons, 263.

Christy, William, Clerk of Quarter Sessions Court, 72; first Auditor of Accounts of Missouri, 244; first Register of Lands, 187; Master, Missouri No. 12, 189; member St. Louis No. 111, 187; military service of, 63; organizer newspaper, 58.

Church, the, preceded by Masonry, 5.

Claiborne, Thomas, first Grand Master of Tennessee, 202.

Clark, James, member Louisiana No. 109, 158.

Clark, William, arrangements for burial of, 183; Brigadier General of Territory Militia, 71; built meeting place for Missouri No. 12, 186; burial at St. Louis, 19; expedition to Prairie du Chien, 64; Governor of Louisiana Territory, 12, 187; initiate of St. Louis, No. 111, 181; joined Missouri Fur Co., 24; Masonic funeral service of, 185; member Missouri No. 12, 189; member St. Louis No. 111, 187; Superintendent of Indian Affairs, 187.

Clarke, Robert P., delegate Missouri State Convention, 232; on Legislative Committee of State Constitution, 233.

Clarkson, William, received degrees in Missouri No. 12, 190.

Clay, Henry, signed act creating Missouri Territory, 12; duel with Humphrey Marshall, 79; Grand Master of Kentucky Grand Lodge, 12, 198; offered resolution in Grand Lodge against dueling, 77; Speaker in House of Representatives, 12.

Cody, "Buffalo Bill," scout and pioneer in Southwest, 23.

Connor, Jeremiah, Erin Benevolent Society organized at his home, 73; member St. Louis No. 111, 178, 187; officer in Missouri No. 12, 187; Sheriff of Court of Common Pleas, 72.

Converse, Seth, Senior Warden in Joachim No. 25, 220.

Cook, Nathaniel, delegate Missouri State Convention, 232; Judicial Committee of State Constitution, 233; member Louisiana No. 109, 156, 168; military service of, 63.

Coons, John, Junior Warden St. Louis No. 111, 182; member St. Louis No. 111, 187; member Territorial Assembly, 187; organizer St. Louis No. 111, 172.

Craig, J., organizer of Grand Lodge of Missouri, 253.

INDEX

Craighead, Alexander, member Louisiana No. 109, 168.
Creath, William, founded "Indiana Patriot," 59.
Criddle, Edward, received degrees Unity No. 6, 229.
Crittenden, T. T., Attorney General of Missouri Territory, 71; member Louisiana No. 109, 168.
Cross, John, organized Unity No. 6, 227.
Cross, Joseph, composed Masonic ode, 178; military service of, 179.
Crow, Albion T., organized Harmony No. 4, 223.
Cupple, Samuel, first Treasurer Unity No. 6, 227.

Daggett, John D., organizer Missouri Grand Lodge, 253; received degrees in Missouri No. 12, 190.
Daggett, Peter, member Louisiana No. 109, 168.
Dallam, Richard B., Secretary St. Louis No. 20, 183.
Darby, John F., author "Recollections," 266.
Darnielle, Isaac, early visitor at Western Star, 99; lawyer at Kaskaskia, 42.
Daviess, Joseph H., Grand Master Kentucky Grand Lodge, 68, 199; killed at Tippecanoe, 68; military service of, 199; prosecuted Aaron Burr, 199; settled in Kentucky, 199; sword presented to Kentucky Grand Lodge, his, 69.
De Camp, Samuel G. J., organizer Missouri Grand Lodge, 40; settled in St. Louis, 40.
Dodge, Henry, charter member Louisiana No. 109, 149; delegate Missouri State Convention, 232; distinguished in Louisiana Territory, 4; first U. S. Marshal in Missouri, 33; Governor Wisconsin Territory, 33; Indian treaties made by, 33; installed officers Unity No. 6, 32; Master Louisiana No. 109, 155; Master Western Star No. 109, 32; military service, 32, 63; organizer Louisiana No. 109, 122; removed Miami Indians, 33; Senator from Wisconsin, 32; Senior Warden Louisiana No. 109, 147, 148, 155; served in Black Hawk War, 33; Superintendent Indian Affairs, 33.
Dodge, Josiah, early religious worker in Missouri, 61; member Louisiana No. 109, 168.
Donnahoe, John, member Louisiana No. 109, 168.
Douberman, John J., received degrees in Missouri No. 12, 191.
Douglass, Thompson, introduced resolution in Missouri Grand Lodge, 214; Master Missouri No. 12, 189, 191; organizer Missouri Grand Lodge, 253.
Dowlin, James, member Louisiana No. 109, 168.
Dred Scott case, argument of, 50.
Du Bourg, Peter Francis, first Grand Warden Louisiana No. 109, 201.
Duelists:
  Beckes, Parmenas, 79.
  Benton, Thomas H., 82.
  Bond, Shadrach, 88.
  Buckner, Andrew, 86.
  Clay, Henry, 79.
  Crittenden, T. T., 89.
  Farrar, Dr. Bernard G., 80.
  Fenwick, Dr. Walter, 89.
  Geyer, Henry S., 81.
  Jones, Rice, 88.
  Lucas, Charles, 84.
  Ramsey, Capt. Thomas, 81.

Smith, John, "T," 90.
Dunlap, James, member Western Star, 99; expelled from his lodge, 88; shot Rice Jones, 88.
Dunn, Azariah C., in first class of Louisiana No. 109, 149.

Easton, Rufus, Charter Member Western Star No. 707, 187; elected to Congress, 46; first postmaster west of Mississippi, 46, 95; first Senior Warden of Western Star, 98; Junior Warden St. Louis No. 111, 46, 187; law practice in St. Louis, 54; organized St. Louis No. 111, 169; organizer Western Star Lodge, 95, 97; prothonotary of Missouri Territory, 46; settled in Law practice in St. Louis, 46.
Edgar, James, Constitution of Louisiana No. 109, 130; death of, 114; first Master of Western Star, 98, 123; Master of St. Charles No. 28, 212; organized Western Star Lodge, 96.
Elliott, Aaron, applied for dispensation for lodge, 118; Charter member, Louisiana No. 109, 149; first American physician west of Mississippi, 35; Master, Louisiana No. 109, 35, 155; Master St. Louis No. 111, 173; organized Louisiana No. 109, 122; settled in Missouri, 35, 119; signer of petition for dispensation, 36.
Elliott, Charles, member Louisiana No. 109, 168.
Elliott, Elias A., member Louisiana No. 109, 168.
Emmons, Benjamin L., delegate Missouri State Convention, 232; on Legislative Committee of State Constitution, 233; Master St. Charles No. 28, 211; President last Missouri Territorial Council, 73.
Erin Benevolent Society, organization of, 73.
Elter, Dr. P., member Louisiana No. 109, 162.

Farrar, Bernard G., duel with J. A. Graham, 80; first physician in St. Louis Territory, 39, 80; Judge Common Pleas, 187; masonic membership, 39; member St. Louis No. 111, 187; organizer newspaper, 58; settled in St. Louis, 39; surgeon in Benton-Lucas duel, 40.
Farris, Robert P., Circuit Attorney for St. Louis, 53; military service of, 53; received degrees, Missouri No. 12, 190.
Fenwick, Ezekiel, caused duel between W. Fenwick and T. T. Crittenden, 89; Treasurer, Louisiana No. 109, 147, 155.
Fenwick, Walter, killed in duel with T. T. Crittenden, 46, 89; one of first petitioners of Western Star Lodge, 99; settled in Missouri, 37.
Fellows, Hart, received degrees in Missouri No. 12, 191.
Ferguson, Peter, member Missouri No. 12, 189.
Finney, J., member Western Star, 99.
Fleming, Nicholas, member Louisiana No. 109, 158.
Foster, George, member Western Star, 99.
Freemasonry, among military leaders in Missouri, 63; chain of Brotherhood, 3; compulsory creed, 5; crosses the Missouri, 209; denounced by Pope, 14; development in the Mississippi Valley, 5; distinguished members in the Lou-

INDEX

isiana Territory, 4; diverse population to be reconciled, 14; duelists, 75; earliest lodges in Louisiana Territory, 6; editors, 57; encouragement of, 6; first Grand Lodge organized, 6; funeral, first Masonic, 41; gratified at transfer of Louisiana to United States, 9; guide post to religion, 5; helped raise the flag, 7; Illinois, in, 206; Indiana, in, 11, 12, 203; interference with, in Louisiana, 201; introduction into Louisiana Purchase, 6; Kentucky, in, 197; lawyers, 41; lodge meetings in pioneer community, 14; lodges in Missouri, 192; lodges in the wilderness, 3; Louisiana, in, 3, 200; membership in Louisiana Territory, 6; military leaders, 62; ministers, 59; Morgan troubles, 3; Mystic Tie, the, 3; Ohio, in, 200; Oregon Trail, on, 16; pathfinders, 18; physicians, 34; pioneers, 34; political leaders, 62; preceded the Church, 5; proportion of members among pioneers in Louisiana Territory, 3; progress in Louisiana Territory, 15; prominent members in Middle West, 15; Santa Fé Trail, on, 16; secret rites unmolested, 10; State Constitution, and the, 230; story in Louisiana Territory, 15; teachers, 59; Tennessee, in, 201; Territorial Governors, 12; Treaty of Session of Louisiana signed by Masons, 10; undesirable members, 16; work of pioneers, 4.

"Freemasonry Follows the Flag," 5, 18.

Frizzell, Joseph, received degrees, Unity No. 6, 229; settled in Missouri, 226.

Funeral, first Masonic, 41.

Gamble, Archibald, attorney for St. Louis public schools, 32; first Grand Treasurer Missouri Grand Lodge, 254; prominent at Lafayette's reception, 53.

Gamble, Hamilton R., Governor of Missouri, 52; Grand Master Missouri Grand Lodge, 52; Judge Supreme Court of Missouri, 52; Secretary of State for Missouri, 52.

Gannt, E. S., advertisement in St. Louis paper, 38; first Senior Warden Unity No. 6, 228; member Missouri No. 12, 190; military service, 38; organizer Unity No. 6, 227; signed By-Laws Unity No. 6, 38.

Garnier, Joseph, Clerk Supreme Court of Missouri, 178; member Missouri No. 12, 189; organizer Missouri Grand Lodge, 253; organizer St. Louis No. 111, 170, 172; Secretary St. Louis No. 111, 178.

Garraty, Joseph W., member St. Charles No. 28, 212.

Geyer, Henry S., defeated Benton for Senatorship, 50; compiled "Digest of Laws of the Territory," 50; Dred Scott case argued by, 50; first Speaker House of Representatives, 50; fought duel with Kennerly, 81; member Missouri No. 12, 190; military service, 50; U. S. Senator, 50.

Gibson, John, first Master Mason created in Indiana Territory, 11; organized Masonry in Indiana Territory, 11; Secretary of Indiana Territory, 11.

TERRITORIAL MASONRY

Giddings, Rev. Salmon, teacher at St. Genevieve, Mo., 60.
Gilbreath, James, organizer Western Star, 97; Junior Warden Western Star No. 107, 123.
Gouion, John J., member Louisiana No. 109, 168.
Government, Territorial ideals of, 13.
Governors, Territorial, 70.
Grand Jury, first in Missouri, 71.
Grand Lodge:
  Acts against dueling, 75.
  First in Missouri, 15.
  Illinois, 207.
  Indiana, 12, 45, 69, 228, 248.
  Kentucky, 68, 76, 197, 248.
  Louisiana, 200, 248.
  Michigan, 205.
  Missouri, 40, 52, 163, 213, 221, 224, 228.
  Mother of all, 17.
  New formations, 156.
  North Carolina, 202.
  Ohio, 200.
  Pennsylvania, 19, 124, 193.
  Tennessee, 29, 51, 59, 185, 196, 201, 220, 224, 248.
Gray, Joseph F., organizer Unity No. 6, 227.
Grimsley, Thornton, organizer Grand Lodge of Missouri 253; received degrees Missouri No. 12, 190.
Guest, Jonathan, member Missouri No. 12, 190.

Haldeman, Peter, received degrees Missouri No. 12, 191.
Hall, Isaac N., edited newspaper in Missouri, 58.
Hall, Sergeant, member Missouri No. 12, 190; purchased and edited newspaper, 58.
Hanley, Thomas, Secretary Erin Benevolent Society, 73.
Hardin, Hugh, organizer Missouri Grand Lodge, 253.

Harmony Lodge No. 4, located at Louisiana, Mo., 223; petition for dispensation, 224; received first charter granted by Missouri Grand Lodge, 225; revived as Perseverance No. 15, 225.
Harrison, Christopher, first State Lieut. Governor Indiana, 12.
Hay, John, Sr., last British Governor of Upper Canada, 30.
Hay, John, Jr., Masonic membership, 3; member Western Star, 99; organizer St. Louis No. 111, 172; public offices in Cahokia held by, 31; starts for Northwest, 31; supposedly received degrees in Missouri No. 12, 191.
Hayes, Henry, member St. Charles No. 28, 212.
Hays, John, fur trader in Mississippi, 31; Indian agent, 31; Masonic membership, 32, 99; organizer St. Louis No 111, 172; postmaster at Cahokia, 31; received degrees Unity No. 6, 229; settled in Cahokia, 31; sheriff St. Clair Co., 31.
Henry, Andrew, fur trader among Indians, 23; Indian attacks on, 24; joined Missouri Fur Co., 24; member Lodges in Missouri, 23; one of first petitioners of Western Star, 99; organizer Louisiana No. 109, 122, 149; Senior Warden Louisiana No. 109, 155; settled in Missouri, 25.
Henry, Isaac N., printer Missouri State Constitution, 236; representative Missouri No. 12 at Tennessee Grand Lodge, 189.
Hepburn, John, organizer Louisiana No. 109, 122.
Herculaneum, location of Joachim No. 25, 220.

INDEX

Hertrick, Joseph, leader among Missouri teachers, 59; military service, 64; Treasurer Louisiana No. 109, 155.

Hickman, William, charter member Louisiana No. 109, 149, 168.

Hoffman, David B., member Missouri No. 12, 190; officer in "St. Louis Guards," 65.

Honey, John W., one of first Deacons of Missouri Grand Lodge, 254.

Hopkins, William H., member Missouri No. 12, 190; organizer Missouri Grand Lodge, 253.

Howland, Daniel, probably member St. Charles No. 28, 212.

Hubbard, Simon M., member Louisiana No. 109, 168.

Hughes, William, received degrees in Missouri No. 12, 191.

Hunt, Harvey, organizer Missouri Grand Lodge, 253.

Hunt, Ezra, first lawyer admitted to bar in Pike Co., 225, 226; Judge in Missouri, 51; master Harmony No. 4, 51; organizer Harmony No. 4, 223.

Illinois, Anti-Masonic agitation, 207; early lodges in, 17; Grand Lodge formed, 207.

Immell, Mich'l, organizer St. Louis No. 111, 172.

Indiana, first Lodge organized at Vincennes, 203; first Master Mason created in, 11; first State Governor, 12; Grand Lodge formed, 204; last Territorial Governor, 12; laws enacted at Vincennes, 11; laws written, 42; Masonic membership in, 204; Masonry organized in, 11; organized as a State, 12; Territory organized, 66; Upper Louisiana attached to, 11; Vincennes, capital of Territory, 11, 66.

Indian treaties, 28.

Iong, Thomas T., Treasurer Louisiana No. 109, 155.

Iowa, early Lodges in, 17.

Irwin, David, Junior Grand Warden Tennessee Grand Lodge, 189.

Israel, Israel, issued dispensation to Western Star, 97.

Jackard, ——, member St. Louis No. 20, 183.

Jackson, Andrew, defeated British at New Orleans, 64; Grand Master Tennessee Grand Lodge, 202; introduced Lafayette to his own Lodge, 203; quarreled with Thomas H. Benton, 82.

James, Phineas, received degrees in Missouri No. 12, 191.

Janis, J. B., Junior Warden Louisiana No. 109, 155.

January, Lawrence A., organizer Harmony No. 4, 223.

Jefferson, Thomas, purchased Louisiana Territory, 10.

Jennings, Jonathan, first Governor of Indiana, 12.

Joachim Lodge, dispensation issued by Tennessee Grand Lodge, 220; founded, 220; helped to form Missouri Grand Lodge, 246; joined Missouri Grand Lodge, 221; located at Herculaneum, Mo., 220; membership, 221; No. 25 on Tennessee register, 220; No. 2 on Missouri register, 221; officers of, 220; stricken from Grand Lodge books, 222; work of the year, 221.

Johnson, Gen. W., brought Masonry to Indiana, 203.

Jones, John, member Louisiana No. 109, 169; one of first Deacons of Missouri Grand

Lodge, 254; organizer of Missouri Grand Lodge, 253; received degrees in Missouri No. 12, 191.
Jones, John Rice, delegate Missouri State Convention, 232; description of, 42; first lawyer in Illinois, 87; first lawyer in territory east of the Mississippi, 42; helped form laws for Louisiana Territory, 11; Judge Missouri Supreme Court, 42; Masonic membership, 42; member Missouri No. 12, 190; member State Constitutional Convention, 42; military service, 42; on Legislative Committee of State Constitution, 233; trustee Missouri Academy, 60.
Jones, Michael, first Junior Warden Western Star, 98; organizer Western Star Lodge, 96.
Jones, Rice, duel with Shadrach Bond, 88; representative in Indiana Territory Legislature, 88; shot by Dr. Dunlap, 88.
Jones, Theodore, received degrees in Unity No. 6, 229.
Judges, Territorial, 72.

Kansas, early lodges in, 17.
Kaskaskia, first Lodge in Missisippi Valley, 118.
Keil, Henry, adjusted Lodge difficulties, 158, 163; Master Louisiana Lodge No. 109, 37; Secretary Louisiana No. 109, 155; Senior Warden Louisiana No. 109, 155.
Keithley, Samuel, probably member St. Charles No. 28, 212.
Kennerly, James, first Senior Grand Warden Missouri Grand Lodge, 254; organizer Grand Lodge of Missouri, 253; received degrees in Missouri No. 12, 190.

Kentucky, establishment of Masonry in, 198; formation of first Lodge, 198; Grand Lodge formed, 198; Murray, William, first Grand Master, 198.
Kimball, Joseph, one of first initiates in Louisiana No. 109, 149; organizer St. Louis No. 111, 170, 172.
Kline, Edward, Senior Warden St. Louis No. 20, 183.
Kneeland, David, received degrees in Missouri No. 12, 191.

Laclede, Pierre Liguest, founder of St. Louis, 27.
Lafayette, received honorary Masonic degrees, 192; visited Missouri Grand Lodge, 53; visited Missouri Chapter No. 1, 4, 191.
Lane, Hardage, Grand Master, 39; member Legislature, 38.
Lane, Harvey, member Louisiana No. 109, 169.
Lassous, Louis, charter member Louisiana No. 109, 149, 169; organizer Louisiana No. 109, 122.
Lavielle, Joseph C., member Missouri No. 12, 190.
"Laws of the Territory of Louisiana," first book printed in Territory, 58.
Lawyers, Pioneer, 41.
Lee, D. F., member St. Louis No. 20, 183.
Le Neve, William, received degrees in Missouri No. 12, 191.
Letcher, Isaac A., organizer Missouri Grand Lodge, 253.
Lewis, Meriwether, application for Dispensation, 19; first Master St. Louis No. 111, 19, 179; formed St. Louis No. 111, 170; Governor Louisiana Territory, 12; headed party to explore Missouri River,

20; inscription on his monument, 181; length of trip to West, 22; letter of credit, 20; Lewis Co., Tenn., formed, 180; lost his life in Tennessee, 180; Masonic membership, 19; monument erected to memory, 180; mustering of Missouri troops, 64; organizer St. Louis No. 111, 172; raised U. S. flag in Louisiana Territory, 9; reached Kentucky on first expedition, 20; recruiting service in Charlottesville, 19; secretary to Pres. Jefferson, 10, 20.
Lewis and Clark, explorations west of Mississippi, 13, 19; in history of Louisiana Territory, 4.
Linn Lewis, eulogy delivered by Benton, 36; Masonic membership, 36, 162; medical practice begun, 36; U. S. Senator from Missouri, 36.
Livingston, Robert R., signer of Treaty of Cession, 10.
Long, William L., received degrees in Missouri No. 12, 190.
Lodges: Abraham (Ky.), 203; American Union No. 4 (Ohio), 200, 204; Boonville No. 14 (Mo.), 232; Cincinnati No. 12, 81, 192; Concord (Md.), 184; Cumberland No. 8 (Tenn.), 202; Franklin Union No. 7 (Mo.), 39, 52, 54; Greenville No. 3 (Tenn.), 202; Harmony No. 4 (Mo.), 51, 193, 223, 247; Hiram No. 3 (Mo.), 214; Hiram No. 4 (Ky.), 39; Hiram No. 7 (Tenn.), 202; Hiram No. 23 (Mo.), 217; Indiana No. 39, 184; in the Wilderness, 3; Joachim (Mo.), 192, 220, 246; King Solomon No. 6 (Tenn.), 202; La Charité No. 93, 200; La Concorde No. 117 (La.), 200; L'Aménité No. 73 (La.), 188; La Parfaite Union No. 29, (S. C.), 200; La Perseverance No. 118 (La.), 200; L'Etoile Polaire No. 129 (La.), 200; Lexington No. 25 (Ky.), 198; Louisiana No. 109, 22, 26, 32, 35, 38, 43, 45, 90, 100, 115, 117, 193, 232, 246; Louisiana No. 111, 193; meetings in pioneer communities, 14; Melchisedec No. 17 (La.), 99; Meriwether Lewis' (Mo.), 49; Missouri No. 1, 29, 39, 40, 41, 48, 50, 53, 54, 56, 63, 183; Missouri No. 11, 58; Missouri No. 12, 29, 42, 49, 50, 54, 56, 59, 71, 73, 81, 186, 192, 232, 246; Newport No. 4 (Tenn.), 202; No. 9 (Philadelphia), 96; No. 13 (Virginia), 22; No. 45 (Pittsburgh), 96; No. 84 (Pa.), 100; Old Franklin (Mo.), 30; Olive Branch (Mo.), 255; Overton No. 5 (Tenn.), 202; Palestine No. 241 (Mo.), 217; Perseverance No. 15 (Mo.), 225; Potomac No. 5 (D. C.), 184; Potosi No. 39 (Mo.), 193, 219, 247; Pre-Grand-Lodge, 218; Registerstown (Md.), 100; Roman No. 82 (N. Y.), 46, 95, 97; St. Andrew's No. 2 (Quebec), 96; St. Charles No. 28 (Mo.), 192, 211, 232, 246; St. Genevieve (Mo.), 32, 59; St. Louis No. 20, 19, 183; St. Louis No. 111, 11, 12, 19, 24, 39, 47, 58, 63, 116, 170, 246, 258; St. Paul's No. 54 (N. Y.), 88; Solomon No. 30 (Va.), 99; Stanton No. 13, 96; Tennessee No. 2, 202; Traveling, 11; Tucker No. 13 (Mo.), 163, 232; Union No. 40 (Conn.), 100; Unity No. 6 (Mo.), 32, 37, 38, 45, 59, 192, 227, 232, 247; Vin-

cennes No. 1 (Ind.), 69, 86, 203; Western Star No. 9 (Tenn.), 202; Western Star No. 107, 22, 23, 81, 88, 89, 92, 122, 232; Western Star No. 109, 32, 37; west of the Mississippi, 16; Widow's Son (Va.), 19.

Louisiana Lodge No. 109, application for Dispensation, 118, 121; approved formation of St. Louis No. 111, 172; By-Laws of, 131; charge for Warrant, 126; Charter forfeited, 159; charter members, 149; Charter received from Missouri Grand Lodge, 163; degrees conferred, 149; dues not sent to Grand Lodge, 154; duration of Lodge, 167; election of officers, 147; first Grand Master, 201; formation of, 119; funds sent to Grand Lodge, 153; Grand Lodge formed, 200, 246; initiations, 149, 152; instructions for constituting new Lodge, 129; Junior Wardens of, 155; Kaskaskia, first Lodge in Mississippi Valley, 118; last payment to Pennsylvania Grand Lodge, 156; letters to Pennsylvania Grand Lodge, 157; Masonry interfered with, 201; Masters of, 155; meeting place, 177; membership list, 148, 155, 1C3; minutes of Pennsylvania Grand Lodge, 124; Mother of all Missouri Lodges, 120; negligence in paying dues, 157; officers of the Lodge, 155; payments to Grand Lodge, 150; petition for reinstatement, 157, 161; prominent members, 167; Report of Committee on By-Laws, 146; reports to Grand Lodge, 150, 152; returns to Grand Lodge, 147; Secretaries of, 155; Senior Wardens of, 155; Story of, 117; Treasurers of, 155; Tucker No. 13, new name of, 163; waiver of jurisdiction by Western Star, 122; Warrant granted, 127.

Louisiana Territory: American Fur Co. in the, 4; Arkansas District created, 12; Kit Carson's exploits in, 4; dissatisfaction of diverse population, 13; distinguished names in history of, 4; earliest Lodges in, 6; early population, 2; French flag hauled down, 8; fur trading in, 13; Grand Lodge, first in, 6; immortalization in novels, 2; Indian uprisings, 63, 65; introduction of Masonry, 6; Lafayette visited St. Louis, 4; land titles created dissension, 14; laws enacted at Vincennes, 11; "Laws of the Territory of Louisiana" published, 12; Lewis and Clark explorations, 4, 13; location of, 1; Masonry helped raise U. S. flag in, 7; Masonry in, 3; Masonry preceded the Church, 5; Morgan troubles, 3; New Madrid District, 12; Oregon Trail, story of, 2; Zebulon Pike's explorations, 4; population of settlements, 13; present membership in, 6; printing of first book in, 12; progress of Masonry in, 15; purchased by Pres. Jefferson, 10; reading the family Bible, 5; religious liberty in, 9; St. Louis the eastern outpost, 2; Secretary of, first, 11; Stoddard, first Governor of, 9; Treaty of Cession of, 10; U. S. flag raised in, 9; Upper Louisiana attached to Indiana, 11; value of work of Freemasonry in, 4.

Lucas, Charles, duel with T. H. Benton, 84.

McArthur, John, first Clerk of Missouri House, 244; member Louisiana No. 109, 169; military service, 63; Treasurer Louisiana No. 109, 148, 155.

McClenahan, Josiah, member Louisiana No. 109, 169.

McFerron, Joseph, delegate Missouri State Convention, 232; entered protest against State Constitution, 241; first Junior Warden Unity No. 6, 228; fought duel with Ogle, 92; member State Convention, 92; organizer Unity No. 6, 227; organizer Western Star, 96; worked for public schools of Missouri, 60.

McGrady, Israel, member Louisiana No. 109, 169.

MacLemore, J. C., Grand Treasurer Tennessee Grand Lodge, 189.

McNair, Alexander, delegate Missouri State Convention, 232; first Governor of Missouri, 178, 187, 243; member Missouri No. 12, 189; member St. Louis No. 111, 178; military service, 63; Master St. Louis No. 111, 187; sheriff Missouri Territory, 72.

Magenis, Arthur, framer of laws for Erin Benevolent Society, 73.

Magennis, A. L., attorney in St. Louis, 54.

Maguire, ——, member St. Louis No. 20, 183.

Marbois, Barbe, French signer of Treaty of Cession, 11.

Martin, James, member Louisiana No. 109, 169.

Mason, Richard, had first Masonic funeral, 41; settled in Missouri, 41.

Master Mason, first created in Indiana Territory, 11.

Mathias, ——, member St. Louis No. 20, 183.

Melody, George H. C., installed first officers in Illinois Grand Lodge, 208; member Missouri No. 12, 190; organizer Missouri Grand Lodge, 253; Treasurer St. Louis No. 20, 183.

Michauz, Andre, accompanied Lewis on first expedition, 20.

Military leaders: Austin, Stephen F., 63; Bartholomew, Gen., 69; Beckes, Benjamin, 69; Beckes, Parmenas, 69; Benton, Thos. H., 63; Bruce, Amos J., 64; Bruff, Maj. J., 62; Buntin, Robert, Sr., 65; Chouteau, Pierre, Jr., 64; Christy, Wm., 63; Clark, Wm., 63; Cook, Nathaniel, 63; Daviess, Joseph H., 68; Dodge, Henry, 63; Hertick, Joseph, 63; Hoffman, David B., 65; Jackson, Andrew, 64; McArthur, John, 63; McNair, Alexander, 63; Oliver, Thomas, 63; Owen, Abraham, 69; Perkins, Joseph, 64; Rector, Stephen, 65; Renshaw, William, 64; Riddick, Thomas F., 63; Scott, John, 63; Shrader, Otho, 64; Simonds, Nathaniel, 63; St. Clair, Gen., 65; Taylor, Waller, 69; White, Isaac, 69; Wilkinson, Benjamin, 64.

Miller, Andrew, member Louisiana No. 109, 169.

Millard, Josiah, charter member Louisiana No. 109, 149, 169.

Ministers, Pioneers, 59.

Mississippi Valley, development of Masonry in, 5.

Missouri, admitted as State, 12, 245; Bill of Rights Committee, 233; Committee on Banks and Banking, 235; Committee on Engrossment and Enrollment, 235; Committee on Printing, 236; Committee on Style, 235; Committee to draft Constitution, 233; Constitution translated into French, 241; early settlements in, 13; election of delegates to State Convention, 231; election of State officers, 243; Executive Committee of State Constitution, 233; first meeting of Legislature, 244; Judicial Committee of State Constitution, 233; last official act of State Convention, 242; Legislative Committee of State Constitution, 233; Mansion House, scene of State Convention, 231; Masonic delegates to State Convention, 232; Masonic neighbors of, 196; population in 1820, 230; prominent in Masonic annals, 16; special sections of State Constitution, 237; special session of Legislature, 245; State Constitution, 233; State government created, 193; story of the convention, 232; Territory created, 12; votes on special sections of State Constitution, 238.

Missouri, Grand Lodge of, By-Laws adopted, 255; Charters issued, 255; Constitution of, 252; Dispensations granted, 255; election of officers, 254; expenses first year, 256; first in Missouri Territory, 246; formation of, 247; foundation of, 15; installation of officers, 254; Lodges composing, 246; meeting of delegates, 253; meeting of Lodges, 249; membership, 256; reasons for organizing, 248; receipts first year, 255; subordinate Lodges, 17; troubles of, 257; withdrawal from Mother Grand Lodge, 250.

Missouri Fur Company, organized by Freemasons, 24, 29.

Missouri Lodge No. 12, degrees conferred by, 190; feasts celebrated, 192; formation of, 188; funeral services, first, 192; helped to form Missouri Grand Lodge, 246; meeting place erected for, 191; roster of members, 189.

Monroe, James, signed Treaty of Cession, 10.

Moore, James, member Western Star, 99.

Moreau, Louis Lasouse, member Western Star, 99.

Morrison, James, endowed professorship in Transylvania university, 198; founded Ky. Bible Society, 198; Grand Master Kentucky Grand Lodge, 198.

Morton, George, received degrees in Missouri No. 12, 190.

Mother Lodge of Mississippi Valley, 94.

"Mother of Grand Lodges," 17.

Mulligan, Charles, organizer Unity No. 6, 227.

Murray, William, Attorney General of Kentucky, 198; prosecuted inquiry into Burr conspiracy, 198.

Mystic Tie, The, in Louisiana Territory, 3.

Neale, Thomas, Masonic membership, 37; organizer Unity No. 6, 227; settled in Missouri, 37.

Neale, William, received degrees Unity No. 6, 229.

Nebraska, early lodges in, 17.

Neighbors, of Missouri Masonic, 196.

New Madrid District, division of, 12.

INDEX

New Mexico, early lodges in, 17.
Newspapers, in the Territory, 57.
Northwest Territory, Legislative Council of, 11.
Norvell, Joshua, editor of "Western Journal," 58; organizer of Missouri No. 12, 188.
Noyes, Michael J., organizer Harmony No. 4, 223; settled in Missouri, 226.

Ohio, first Grand Master, 200; Grand Lodge formed, 200; six lodges formed, 200.
Oklass, John, member Louisiana No. 109, 158.
Oliver, Thomas, charter member Louisiana No. 109, 149; Junior Warden Louisiana No. 109, 155; member Western Star, 99; military service of, 63; organizer Louisiana No. 109, 122; Secretary Louisiana No. 109, 147, 155; Secretary St. Louis No. 111, 173.
O'Neill, Hugh, organizer of Erin Benevolent Society, 74.
Owen, Abraham, killed at Tippecanoe, 69.
Owen, Benjamin, member St. Charles No. 28, 212.

Palmer, Bennett, Senior Warden St. Charles No. 28, 211.
Pathfinders, 18.
Paul, Gabriel, member St. Louis No. 111, 188.
Paul, René, member St. Louis No. 111, 188.
Payne, John, Junior Warden St. Charles No. 28, 211.
Penrose, James H., member St. Charles No. 28, 212; organizer Missouri Grand Lodge, 253; received degrees in Missouri No. 12, 190.

Perdreauville, René, member St. Louis No. 111, 188.
Perkins, Joseph, lieutenant in Indian expedition, 64; member first Grand Jury in St. Louis, 29; member Louisiana No. 109, 169; organizer Missouri Fur Co., 29.
Pettit, Jacob, member Louisiana No. 109, 169.
Pettus, William G., delegate to convention to form Grand Lodge, 213; engrossed Missouri State Constitution, 242; surveyor of St. Louis Co., 73; Master Hiram No. 3, 216; member Missouri No. 12, 190; member St. Charles No. 28, 212; organizer Missouri Grand Lodge, 253; Secretary of Missouri State Convention, 232; secretary to first Governor of Missouri, 244.
Phelan, James C., organizer Harmony No. 4, 223.
Physicians, Pioneer, 34.
Pike, Zebulon, explorations of, 4, 13, 22.
Pike's Peak, discovery of, 22.
Pilcher, Joshua, familiar with Northwest Territory, 29; Master Missouri No. 12, 29; organizer Missouri Fur Co., 29; organizer Missouri No. 12, 188; second at Benton-Lucas duel, 29; Supt. Indian Affairs, 29.
Pinkley, Henry, member Louisiana No. 109, 169.
Pioneers: *Editors:* Alexander, Walter, 59; Charles, Joseph, 57; Creath, William, 59; Hall, Sergeant, 58; Henry, Isaac N., 58; Norvell, Joshua, 58; Russell, James, 59; Whitney, Minor M., 59. *Lawyers:* Bates, Edward, 54; Bent, Silas, 49; Benton, Thomas H., 56; Berry, Taylor, 54; Buckner, Alexander, 44; Bul-

litt, George, 45; Carr, Wm. C., 48; Crittenden, T. T., 45; Easton, Rufus, 46; Farris, Robert P., 53; Gamble, Archibald, 53; Gamble, Hamilton R., 52; Geyer, Henry S., 50; Hunt, Ezra, 51; Jones, John Rice, 42; Magennis, A. L., 54; Redd, William J., 54; Ryland, John F., 51; Scott, John, 43, 55; Stuart, Alexander, 47; Tucker, Nathanial B., 47; Wash, Robert, 52. *Ministers and Teachers:* Boon, Hampton, 61; Bullitt, George, 59; Bynum, Grey, 60; Dodge, Henry, 59; Elliott, Aaron, 59; Fenwick, Walter, 59; Giddings, Rev. Salmon, 60; Henry, Andrew, 59; Hertick, Joseph, 59; Kiel, Henry, 59; McFerron, Joseph, 60; Oliver, Thomas, 59; Riddick, Thomas F., 60; Scott, Aaron, 59; Scott, John, 60; Shepherd, Elihu H., 60; Ward, Rev. John, 60; Williams, Justinian, 61. *Pathfinders:* Carson, Kit, 23; Berthold, Bartholomew, 26; Bridger, James, 30; Bent, Charles, 23; Cabanne, John, 27; Chouteau, Pierre, Jr., 27; Clark, William, 19; Cody, "Buffalo Bill," 23; Columbia Fur Co., 28; Dodge, Henry, 32; Hay, John, 30; Henry, Andrew, 23; Lewis, Meriwether, 19; Missouri Fur Co., 29; Pike, Zebulon M., 22; Pratte, Father and Son, 27; Robinson, Dr. John H., 22; St. Vrain, Ceran, 23; Waldo, David, 23. *Physicians:* DeCamp, Samuel G. J., 40; Elliott, Aaron, 35; Farrar, Bernard G., 39; Fenwick, Ezekiel, 37; Fenwick, Walter, 37; Gannt, Edw. S., 38; Lane, Hardage, 38; Linn, Lewis, 36; Neale, Thomas, 37; Robinson, Dr. John H., 40.

Platt, Abraham S., delegate State Convention, 213; organizer Missouri Grand Lodge, 253; probably member St. Charles No. 28, 212.

Pocock, W. H., organizer Missouri Grand Lodge, 253.

Political Leaders, 62.

Posey, Thomas, defeated for State governor, 12; last Territorial governor of Indiana, 12.

Postmaster, first, west of Mississippi River, 46.

Potosi Lodge, Charter granted, 219; helped to form Missouri Grand Lodge, 247; petition for Lodge, 219.

Potter, John C., organizer Missouri Grand Lodge, 253.

Potts, Nathaniel R., on Committee of By-Laws of Louisiana No. 109, 147.

Pratte, Bernard, Dr., member American Fur Co., 27.

Pratte, Bernard, Jr., Associate Judge Common Pleas, 72; delegate Missouri State Convention, 232; member American Fur Co., 27.

Pre-Grand-Lodge Lodges, 218.

Price, Risdon H., lieutenant first volunteer militia in St. Louis, 64; member Missouri No. 12, 189; member St. Louis No. 111, 187.

Prince, William, first sheriff Indiana Territory, 69; served at Tippecanoe, 69.

Pusey, Nathan, member Louisiana No. 109, 169.

Putnam, Rufus, first Grand Master Ohio Grand Lodge, 200.

Querey, Charles, member Western Star Lodge, 99.

INDEX

Ramsey, Thomas, fought duel with Captain Martin, 81; Masonic funeral of, 192.
Randolph, Thomas, Attorney General Indiana Territory, 69; killed at Tippecanoe, 69.
Ranken, Robert, organizer Erin Benevolent Society, 74.
Ranney, Johnson, received degrees Unity No. 6, 229.
Rector, Stephen, officer in "St. Louis Guards," 65; received degrees in Missouri No. 12, 190.
Rector, William, delegate Missouri State Convention, 232; on Executive Committee of State Convention, 233; Surveyor General of Missouri, 72.
Redd, William J., Masonic membership of, 54.
Regnier, François, member Louisiana No. 109, 169.
Religious denominations, in Missouri, 61.
Renshaw, William, first Grand Secretary for Missouri Grand Lodge, 254; member Missouri No. 12, 190; officer in "St. Louis Guards," 64; organizer of Grand Lodge of Missouri, 250.
Rice, N., probably in St. Charles No. 28, 212.
Riddick, N., member St. Charles No. 28, 212.
Riddick, Thomas F., business associates of, 261; Clerk Court of Common Pleas, 72; delegate Missouri State Convention, 232; family history, 259; father of Public Schools in Missouri, 266; first Grand Master of Missouri, 29, 254; Grand Master of Missouri Grand Lodge, 99, 186; greatest work with land titles, 265; home in St. Louis, 264; Masonic history, 257, 262, 265; member Missouri No. 12, 189; member Solomon Lodge No. 30 (Va.), 99; military service of, 63, 262; newspaper advertisements of, 264; on Committee on Banks and Banking of Missouri State Constitution, 235; organized Christ Church, St. Louis, 262; organizer Grand Lodge of Missouri, 253; organized Louisiana No. 109, 122; organizer St. Louis No. 111, 170, 172; public offices held by, 260; Senior Warden St. Louis No. 111, 182; work for Public Schools of Missouri, 60.
Roberts, Edmund, member Louisiana No. 109, 169; Secretary of Louisiana No. 109, 155.
Roberts, Edward, Secretary, Louisiana No. 109, 145.
Roberts, William F., Master Joachim No. 25, 220.
Robertson, John H., member Louisiana No. 109, 169.
Robinson, David, prominent in Territorial Freemasonry, 22.
Robinson, John H., accompanied Pike expedition, 22, 41; Masonic membership, 41; member Lodge No. 13 in Virginia, 22; Senior Warden St. Louis No. 111, 41.
Robinson, Robert, organizer Western Star Lodge, 97.
Rocheblave, Philip, demitted from Western Star, 112; received degrees in Missouri No. 12, 191.
Roe, Daniel, member Louisiana No. 109, 169.
Rollins, Henry, received degrees Missouri No. 12, 191.
Royal Arch Masonry, first chapter west of Mississippi, 191; first written record of, in Louisiana Territory, 63;

Missouri Chapter, 39; Vincennes Chapter No. 1, 39.
Rule, William K., received degrees Missouri No. 12, 190.
Russell, James, edited newspaper in Missouri, 59; received degrees Unity No. 6, 229.
Rutter, Edmund, organizer Unity No. 6, 227; settled in Missouri, 226.
Ryland, John F., Grand Master of Missouri, 51; Judge of Missouri Supreme Court, 52; received degrees Missouri No. 12, 190; settled in Missouri to practice law, 51.

St. Charles Lodge No. 28, formed, 211; helped to form Missouri Grand Lodge, 246; Hiram No. 3 under Missouri Grand Lodge, 216; Hiram No. 23, later name of, 217; invited to attend convention for Grand Lodge, 212; membership, 212; officers of, 211; Palestine No. 241, present name of, 217; petition to Missouri Grand Lodge for warrant, 214.
St. Clair, General, defeat by Indiana, 65.
St. Louis Lodge No. 111, application for dispensation, 171; approval of Louisiana No. 109 gained, 172; certificate filed with Grand Secretary, 176; degree conferred, 184; extension of time on dues granted, 195; feasts celebrated, 177; formation of, 171; French flag hauled down, 8; funeral service for Gen. William Clark, 185; helped to form Missouri Grand Lodge, 246; meeting place, 177; newspaper notices, 177; notification of arrears of dues, 195; petition for warrant, 193; prominent members, 170; records lost, 179; reports not made to Grand Lodge, 177; roster of, 186; United States flag raised in, 9.
St. Vrain, Ceran, assisted in opening Great Southwest, 23.
Scott, Andrew, Clerk in last Territorial Assembly, 219; first Master Potosi Lodge, 219; member Louisiana No. 109, 169; trustee of Missouri Academy, 60.
Scott, John, charter member Louisiana No. 109, 149; delegate to Missouri State Convention, 232; early visitor at Western Star, 99; father of public school system of Missouri State Constitution, 240; first member of Congress from Missouri, 99; Junior Warden Louisiana No. 109, 147, 148, 155; Master Louisiana No. 109, 145, 155; member of Congress, 43, 55; military service of, 63; Scott County, Missouri, named for him, 44; Senior Warden Louisiana No. 109, 155; Senior Warden St. Louis No. 111, 173; settled in Missouri, 43; Territorial delegate to Congress from Missouri, 73.
Scott, Moses, member Missouri No. 12, 190.
Searcy, Robert, Grand Master of Tennessee Grand Lodge, 188.
Searcy, William, one of first initiates in Louisiana No. 109, 149; Secretary Louisiana No. 109, 155.
Seavers, Charles, received degrees Unity No. 6, 229.
Setcher, Isaac A., received degrees Missouri No. 12, 190.
Shade, Will G., member St. Charles No. 28, 212.

INDEX 289

Shepherd, Elihu H., prominent among Missouri teachers, 60.
Shrader, Otho, captain of troop of horse in militia, 64; charter member Louisiana No. 109, 149; made remittance to Pennsylvania Grand Lodge, 153; Master Louisiana No. 109, 100, 147, 148, 155; member Lodge No. 84 (Pa.), 100; military service of, 100; organized Louisiana No. 109, 122; Territorial Judge, 71, 119.
Simonds, Nathaniel, member St. Charles No. 28, 212; member of committee to draft Constitution, 213; military service, 63; organizer of Grand Lodge of Missouri, 250.
Smith, John "T," charter member Louisiana No. 109, 149; joined expedition of Aaron Burr, 91; killed Lionel Browne in duel, 90; made best guns in Tennessee, 90; original "bad man" of Missouri, 90; Territorial Judge, 91.
Smith, Reuben, member Louisiana No. 109, 169.
Smith, William, probably in St. Charles No. 28, 212.
Smith, Zenas, received degrees Missouri No. 12, 191.
Southwest, Great, opening of, 23.
Spencer, James F., received degrees Missouri No. 12, 190.
Stark, William, received degrees Missouri No. 12, 191.
Stoddard, Amos, first Governor of Louisiana Territory, 9.
Stoddard, John, member St. Charles No. 28, 212.
Stuart, Alexander, attorney for Lewis, 47; Judge of Circuit Court, 47; member Missouri No. 12, 189; member Virginia Executive Council, 47; Territorial Judge of Illinois, 47.

Tannehill, Wilkins, Grand Secretary of Tennessee Grand Lodge, 189.
Taylor, Samuel, member St. Charles No. 28, 212.
Taylor, Major Waller, served at Tippecanoe, 69.
Teachers, pioneer, 59.
Tennessee, approved by Mother Grand Lodge, 201; deed of relinquishment received from North Carolina Grand Lodge, 202; first Grand Master, 202; Grand Lodge formed, 202.
Terry, Robert, charter member Louisiana No. 109, 149, 169; organizer Louisiana No. 109, 122.
Tholozan, John E., received degrees Missouri No. 12, 191.
Tippecanoe, Battle of, 67.
Tipton, John, donated Tippecanoe battlefield to Indiana, 70; Grand Master Indiana Grand Lodge, 227.
Treaty of Cession, transfer of Louisiana Territory, 10.
Trimble, James, Senior Grand Warden Tennessee Grand Lodge, 189.
Tucker, Nathaniel B., eccentric mode of living, 48; education of, 48; Grand Master of his lodge, 48; law practice in Missouri, 48; member Missouri No. 12, 189.

Unity Lodge No. 6, application for Dispensation, 227; charter granted, 229; degrees conferred, 228; Dispensation issued, 227; helped to form Missouri Grand Lodge, 247; transferred to Missouri Grand Lodge, 228.
Upper Louisiana, attached to Indiana, 11.

Utah, early lodges in, 17.

Valle, Francois, charter member Louisiana No. 109, 149; companion of Major Henry in exploration, 23; member Louisiana No. 109, 169; member Western Star, 99; organizer Louisiana No. 109, 122.
Vance, John G., organized Unity No. 6, 227.
Vanderburgh, Henry, active in Masonry in Indiana, 204; framing laws for Louisiana Territory, 11; Masonic degrees received in New York State, 11; member court to make district laws, 71; President Legislative Council of Northwest Territory, 11; Territorial Judge, 11.
Varner, William, member Louisiana No. 109, 169.
Vincennes, capital of Indiana Territory, 11; territorial laws enacted at, 11.

Waldo, David, one of scouts of Southwest, 23.
Walker, ———, organizer of newspaper, 58.
Walker, Benjamin, probably in St. Charles No. 28, 212.
Wall, Moses B., received degrees Missouri No. 12, 191.
Wallace, John, received degrees Missouri No. 12, 191.
Wallace, Robert, delegate Missouri State Convention, 232.
Walls, John, received degrees Missouri No. 12, 190.
Walters, Joseph, received degrees Missouri No. 12, 191.
Ward, Rev. John, first Episcopalian minister in Missouri, 60; Grand Chaplain Grand Lodge of Kentucky, 262.
Wash, Robert, Attorney General of Missouri, 72; Judge Missouri Supreme Court, 53; member Missouri No. 12, 189; military service of, 53; U. S. Attorney, 53.
Washington, early lodges in, 17.
Watkins, Nathaniel W., received degrees Unity No. 6, 229.
Weber, John H., member Louisiana No. 109, 169.
Welch, Thomas M., member Louisiana No. 109, 169.
Western Lodge No. 107, application for Dispensation, 95; by-laws, 98, 105; certificate and recommendation, 101; charter granted, 103; Committee on By-Laws, 104; dimit granted, 112; diplomas granted, 111; dispensation granted, 97; early visitors reported, 99; feasts celebrated, 113; first petitions received, 99; funeral customs, 114; last meeting recorded, 115; Mother Lodge, 94; minutes of early meeting, 111; name chosen, 98; officers appointed, 104; organization of, 95; renewal of petition, 100; waiver of jurisdiction, 122.
White, Isaac, killed at Tippecanoe, 69.
White, Joseph, organizer of Grand Lodge of Missouri, 253; received degrees Missouri No. 12, 190.
Whitlow, Coleman, member Louisiana No. 109, 169.
Whitney, Minor M., editor of St. Louis paper, 59; received degrees Unity No. 6, 229.
Wilkinson, Benjamin, captain of first volunteer company of militia in St. Louis, 64; organized St. Louis No. 111, 172.
Wilkinson, Walter, member Louisiana No. 109, 169.
Willard, Rowland, member St. Charles No. 28, 212.

Williams, Justinian, early religious worker in Missouri, 61.
Wilson, Andres, member St. Charles No. 28, 212.
Wilson, George, member St. Louis No. 20, 183.
Wilson, Nicholas, member Louisiana No. 109, 169.
Wisconsin, early lodges in, 17.
Wood, James, member Louisiana No. 109, 169.
Woodson, Samuel, offered resolution in Grand Lodge against dueling, 77.

Yard, James M., received degrees Missouri No. 12, 191.
Young, Benjamin, member Western Star Lodge, 99.
Young, Samuel H. T., member Louisiana No. 109, 169; Secretary Louisiana No. 109, 148, 155.

www.ingramcontent.com/pod-product-compliance
Lightning Source LLC
LaVergne TN
LVHW041529230525
812066LV00001B/45